Henry Highland Garnet, James McCune Smith

**A Memorial Discourse**

Henry Highland Garnet, James McCune Smith

**A Memorial Discourse**

ISBN/EAN: 9783337817640

Printed in Europe, USA, Canada, Australia, Japan

Cover: Foto ©Thomas Meinert / pixelio.de

More available books at **www.hansebooks.com**

A

# MEMORIAL DISCOURSE;

BY

## REV. HENRY HIGHLAND GARNET,

DELIVERED IN THE HALL OF THE HOUSE OF REPRESENTATIVES,

WASHINGTON CITY, D. C.

ON SABBATH, FEBRUARY 12, 1865.

WITH AN

# INTRODUCTION.

BY

## JAMES McCUNE SMITH, M. D.

PHILADELPHIA:
JOSEPH M. WILSON.
1865.

STEREOTYPED BY WESTCOTT & THOMSON, PHILADELPHIA.

Henry Highland Garnet

# CORRESPONDENCE.

WASHINGTON, D. C., Feb. 14. 1865.

To the REV. HENRY HIGHLAND GARNET.

DEAR SIR:—We, the undersigned, and many others of your fellow-citizens. who had the pleasure of hearing your eloquent sermon preached in the HOUSE OF REPRESENTATIVES OF THE UNITED STATES, on SUNDAY MORNING, FEBRUARY THE 12TH, do respectfully request a copy for publication, together with a sketch of your life.

As you are the first colored man who has on any occasion spoken in our National Capitol, and as you spoke so ably for God and universal liberty, we regard the event as worthy of note, and desire to hand it down to posterity as an important epoch in our history.

Yours respectfully,

| | | |
|---|---|---|
| THOMAS R. FOOTE, | F. R. BURTON, | JOHN H. DIGGS. |
| URIAH DALY, | J. P. S. SCHUREMAN, | GURDON SNOWDON, |
| W. H. WHEELER. | C. REMOND DOUGLASS, | A. WATSON, |
| WM. H. STEPHENS. | WILLIAM B. ELLIS, | J. E. GREEN, |
| J. O. BUTLER, | J. S. WORMLEY, | C. C. TILLMAN, |
| CARTER A. STEWART, | A. R. ABBOTT. | A. L. BRYAN, |
| HERBERT HARRIS, | THOS. S. BOSTON, | ROYAL H. BROWN, |
| N. B. MYERS. | S. F. JOHNSON, | WM. J. FOLSON, |
| COLBERT S. SYPHAX. | JOHN A. GRAY, | D. E. WYCOFF, |
| J. MARSHALL, | SAMUEL PEIRCE, | JOHN W. RAPIER, |
| CHARLES E. MILLER, | F. R. FREEMAN. | JAS. B. MARTIN, |
| WM. F. LANDRE, | CHAS. H. M. WOOD, | SAMUEL J. DATCHER. |
| L. A. CORNISH. | G. W. WILKINSON, | |

WASHINGTON, D. C.. March 15th. 1865.

To MESSRS. THOMAS R. FOOTE. THOMAS S. BOSTON, URIAH DALY. S. J. JOHNSON, and others.

GENTLEMEN:—I am truly grateful to you for the favor and approbation with which you have been pleased to regard my humble effort on the occasion to which you refer. Relying upon your judgment, rather than upon my own, I will comply with your request.

I am yours truly,

HENRY HIGHLAND GARNET.

WASHINGTON, D. C., March 31, 1865.

At a meeting of the Elders and Trustees of the Fifteenth Street Presbyterian Church, Washington City, D. C., the following preamble and resolutions were adopted.

*Whereas,* The adoption by Congress of an amendment to the Constitution of the United States, abolishing slavery forever throughout our land, is an event so important, and fraught with so much interest to the nation as to call forth our profoundest gratitude to God, and

*Whereas,* The Chaplain of the House of Representatives, Rev. WM. H. CHANNING, together with a number of the Republican members of the House, believing that it would be eminently wise and proper to have some public religious service to commemorate such an auspicious event, requested our pastor, Rev. HENRY HIGHLAND GARNET, to deliver a memorial discourse on the second Sabbath of February, 1865. Therefore

*Resolved,* That the thanks of the congregation be tendered to those members of the Senate and House of Representatives who voted for said amendment.

*Resolved,* That our thanks are due to Rev. William H. Channing for courtesies to our pastor.

*Resolved,* That whilst we see the hand of God leading us in the present crisis of our nation's history, we feel grateful to him for having raised up that noble band of Abolitionists who for more than a generation have lifted up their voices in behalf of the oppressed, and in favor of freedom.

*Resolved,* That the Memorial Discourse delivered on said occasion be published, and that Dr. JAMES McCUNE SMITH, of New York, be requested to prepare a sketch of the life of our pastor.

Signed on behalf of the congregation by

CHARLES BRUCE, WILLIAM SLADE, EDWARD CRUSOR, DAVID FISHER, WM. J. WILSON, } *Ruling Elders.*

WALKER LEWIS, ALFRED KIGER, JNO. F. COOK, S. G. BROWN, WM. H. SHORTER, HENRY F. GRANT, A. O. JONES, HENRY PIPER. } *Trustees.*

# SKETCH OF THE LIFE AND LABORS

## OF

# REV. HENRY HIGHLAND GARNET.

---

HENRY H. GARNET was born on the 23d December, 1815, at New Market, Kent Co., Maryland.

His ancestry did not come over in the May-Flower, nor land at Plymouth Rock, nor kiss the blarney stone of the Pilgrim Fathers. On the contrary, his grandfather was stolen by slave-traders from the coast of Africa, survived the horrors of the middle-passage, on a ship doubtless owned in Bristol or Boston, landed on the James River, and was thence transferred to the estate of Colonel William Spencer at New Market, doomed to perpetual slavery, himself and his heirs forever; himself, according to REV. DR. SEABURY, in exchange for the life forfeited in battle, and his offspring forever, according to the same luminous authority, by what may be termed the "baby contract."*

And yet this grandfather, shorn of his strength and bound with bands of steel, "was as noble an ancestor as human kind could desire." Of

---

* "We have seen that the contract which tacitly subsists between the master and his slaves, devolves on the one party the care and protection, and on the other party the duty of service. Now the children of slaves are naturally part of their parents —bone of their bone, and flesh of their flesh. Naturally, therefore, as well as justly, and by a moral necessity, they become parties to the contract that subsists between their parents and the master. (How, O learned Doctor, does this contract read, when one of the parents *is* the master?) That infants as soon as born, are incapable of becoming parties to a contract, will be affirmed by no person who is even moderately conversant with moral science."—*American Slavery Justified:* by DR. SEABURY, p. 160.

3

nearly perfect physical make-up, he survived unscathed that middle-passage whose horrors soon roused Clarkson and Wilberforce to compass its destruction; and along with physical he brought moral and religious power with him to New Market, which won for him the significant name of Joseph Trusty,—JOSEPH from his gifts in exhorting, praying, and praising the Lord, and TRUSTY from his unbending integrity of character.

In due course of time there were added to the family of Joseph Trusty six stalwart sons and two daughters, between whom and Colonel Spencer, the owner of the estate, there was doubtless executed the "contract" of Rev. Dr. Seabury's imagination. And from what happened, it would seem that the contract was well kept on both sides. Colonel Spencer, a "high-toned," liberal gentleman, rejoicing in his human chattels, bestowed every care and attention on their food, clothing, and other comforts, and took great pride in having them appear well. In the further course of time these sons of Joseph Trusty grew up to manhood, and in their turn became fathers of families. George, the son who most resembled his father Joseph in person and character, became the father of Henry H. Garnet, whose mother was a woman of extraordinary energy, industrious, pious, and holding at the highest value that education from which her condition had debarred her, and continued to debar her children.

Col. Spencer, who was a bachelor, died in 1824, devising his estate, real and personal, (including the "baby contracts,") to his brother Isaac and sundry nephews. These heirs took a different view from their testator, of the Patriarchal Institution. They determined to exercise their Constitutional Rights to the fullest extent, and reduce those who had hitherto borne the name of slaves, down, to bear the veriest yoke and degradation of slavery. As they made no secret of their intention, it reached the ears of the Trustys, a portion of whom, headed by Henry's father, held a family council, wherein they opened a new volume, in which, forgetful of "contracts" and constitutional obligations, they made sundry entries treating of their own rights to their own persons, and to the fruits of their own labor: in a word, of their Liberty!

Within a few weeks after the death of Col. Spencer, a family exodus was planned and carried out in the following manner. Permission having been obtained to attend the funeral of a relative at some few miles distance, eleven in number started in the same night on that sad errand ostensibly, but really with hearts which the North Star lit up with its wondrous joys, to the liberty-seeking slave. A covered market wagon awaited them in a piece of woods; they got in and kept on till near daybreak, when they left the wagon and concealed themselves in the woods until night. Henry's father, mother, sister, and seven others, including himself, composed this company. They have not, to this day, returned from that funeral, although all of them, except the subject of this memoir, having bountifully partaken of the blessings of Liberty, are gone on a longer and brighter pilgrimage.

For several days they slept in the woods and swamps, traveling all night long. Henry, now nine years old, kept up with the fugitives, until his little limbs gave out, when his father and uncles took turns in carrying him upon their backs. After weary travel by night and partial rest by day, they at length reached Wilmington, Del., and that ever to be remembered half-way house for pilgrims on the road to Freedom, the barn of Thomas Garret, the good Quaker, the noble-hearted philanthropist, to whom so many thousands of our brethren, on the way to Liberty, are indebted for shelter, aid, and sustenance. In times now remote, one of the kings of England, having lost his queen in a distant part of the realm, started with a solemn and gorgeous funeral procession on his way to her burial-place near London; the progress was slow, and, at the end of each day's march, was a halt until the following morning. In after years, he manifested his profound grief at the loss of his consort, by causing to be erected at each of these resting-places a beautiful and costly cross of most elaborate and beautiful workmanship; some of these yet remain as monuments of royal sorrow and affection. Is it hoping too much, that in "the good time coming," this resting-place of the captive, this first breathing-spot of the budding freeman, this first assured foothold on the free earth, may, in like manner, be consecrated forever, by some sacred fane, in which songs of joy, of ransom and of liberty may be sung forever?

At Wilmington the fugitives separated; seven of the company went into New Jersey, to Greenwich and Salem; Henry's family went to New Hope, Bucks County, Pa., where he first entered a school-house. They remained in Pennsylvania a few months, and then moved to New York.

In 1825, the pilgrims arrived in New York, and life and hope began to bud. Although yet, and for two years after a slave State, there was a safer and more expansive feeling in this State than in Pennsylvania, which had been a free State some thirty years. There was something more gladdening in the State in which freedom was newly entering, than in the other State whose so-called free border was in poisoned contact with the direful institution of slavery.

In the city of New York, as we have said, a new life seemed to open up to our wanderers, and, following the example given in the Holy Scriptures, they took a new name, and called themselves Garnets. The process of this re-baptism, or baptism to Liberty, was simple, solemn, primitive. The father called up the little flock which had escaped from the wolves, and said: "By the blessings of God we are now free—come, let us worship him." Gifted and fervent in prayer, he poured out his whole soul at this homely altar, in which he felt freedom united with religion for the first time in his sojourn on this earth. He then rose from his knees, and said to Henry's mother: "Wife, they used to call you Henny (Henrietta), but in future your name is Elizabeth."

Placing his hand on his daughter's head: "Your name is not Mary any longer, but Eliza." "And, my dear little boy," he continued, taking him on his knees: "Your name is Henry." "My name is George Garnet." With these new names they started anew on the journey of life.

Mr. George Garnet soon found profitable employment in working at his trade, shoe-making. He also exercised his other gifts with so much acceptance, that he rapidly rose in the estimation of his Christian brethren, and became a class-leader and exhorter in the African Methodist Episcopal Church, Bethel, then worshipping in Mott Street.

Henry was sent to the New York African Free School, No. 1, in Mulberry Street, in the year 1826. At this date his public life began. In all cases, the school-house, and school-boy days, settle the permanent characteristics, establish the level, guage the relative, mental, and moral power of the man in after life; especially was it so in this school for ten years before and several years after this date. The colored people of New York, from an early date, carried themselves with a free air which showed that they felt themselves free, and on more than one occasion alarmed their best friends by their bold action. In 1809, at the first anniversary of the African Society for Mutual Relief, they had some very handsome silk banners painted, one of which contained a full-length portrait of one of their number, with the motto:

"Am I not a Man and a Brother?"

With these banners it was understood that they were about to parade the public streets. Their white friends called at the meeting of the Society and protested, begged, insisted that they should not attempt any thing so fool-hardy. Secure in their manhood and will, they did parade, in large number, on the appointed day, easily thrusting aside by their own force the small impediments which blocked their way. This feeling of independence was strengthened by the part taken by this people in the War of 1812–15. And then gradually was added to it the best blood of the South, which drifted this way, in search of freedom, or escaping from attempts at insurrection. Hence, in church meetings, as well as in school-rooms, men, women, and children, embracing the best energies of all the Southern States collided with the sturdy New Yorkers, to glory in giving praise for their escape from the house of bondage, to pray for the downfall of slavery, and to rejoice and press forward the young in the priceless advantages of free schools. The children also took up the burden of their fathers, and their dreams and their plays were of freedom, and they hated the "kidnapper" worse than the father of evil.

African School, No. 2, was then taught by Mr. Charles C. Andrews, an Englishman by birth, of versatile talents; himself not deeply learned, but thorough so far as he went, a good disciplinarian, and in true sympathy with his scholars in their desire to advance. One special habit of his was to find out the bent of his boys, and then, by encouragement, instruction, and, if need were, employing at his own expense additional teachers to develope such talent as far as possible.

In spelling, penmanship, grammar, geography, and astronomy, he rightly boasted that his boys were equal, if not superior, to any like number of scholars in the city, and freely challenged competition at his Annual Examinations. In Natural Philosophy and Navigation, which were then new studies in a free school, he carried on classes as far as he was able, and then hired more competent teachers at his own expense. To stimulate his pupils, and bring out their varied talents, he instituted periodical fairs, at which were exhibited the handiwork of the children, who were rewarded by tickets and those creature comforts which school-boys and girls so well know how to estimate.

Without being, in the modern sense, an abolitionist, Mr. Andrews held that his pupils had as much capacity to acquire knowledge as any other children, they were the object of his constant labors, and it was thought by some, that he even regarded his black boys as a little smarter than whites. He taught his boys and girls to look upward; to believe themselves capable of accomplishing as much as any others could, and to regard the higher walks of life as within their reach. He instituted among the advanced scholars a " CLASS OF MERIT," which was a literary and deliberative assembly, which held periodical meetings for the transaction of business, elected officers, and kept minutes, which may still be found among the archives of the Mulberry Street school.

To this school, and under this teacher, was Henry sent, in 1826, when eleven years old. Among his schoolmates were some, not unknown in their day.

GEORGE R. ALLEN, a little boy, perfectly black, so fragile that you might crush him between thumb and finger, was head-boy in Arithmetic, Natural Philosophy, and Astronomy; he was little less than a prodigy of calculation and original thought on the abstruse problems of gravity, cohesion, and the laws of planetary motion. His knowledge of navigation stood him in good stead some years after, when being at sea, as a sailor, the captain and mate of the vessel, a whaler, both died; the men were at a loss what to do, when George, taking up the sextant, told them he could navigate; at first incredulous, they gladly yielded to his proofs of ability, and he brought the ship safely into New Bedford. Thence he afterwards sailed as second officer of the same vessel; but unfortunately, with all hands she was lost at sea.

IRA ALDRIDGE, a histrionic artist of highest rank who bears the gifts of several European kings, as well as the title of Chevalier.

PATRICK H. REASON, the splendid engraver on steel, also is still in the full tide of his successful artist life. It may as well be recorded here, that the hand of a colored man (Mr. Reason) engraved the massive coffin plate of Daniel Webster.

PROFESSOR CHARLES L. REASON, well known as a most successful teacher, and highly esteemed as a thinker and writer.

REV. ALEXANDER CRUMMELL, M. A., Oxon., whose resistance to caste in the Church is eloquently recorded by Arch-Deacon Wilberforce in his History of Episcopacy in the United States: who is widely known in three continents for his learning, eloquence, and logical power: and who prefers to devote his great talents, so well fitted to adorn the highest walks of civilization, to the enlightening the heathen, and illumining with Gospel light despised and down-trodden Africa.

REV. ISAIAH G. DE GRASSE, the fine scholar and eloquent preacher, cut off in his early prime. Mr. De Grasse also came in contact with caste in the Protestant Episcopal Theological Seminary. Having been admitted regularly, as a student, the fact was bruited about the building, the Southern and dough-faced students raised a clamor, and the trustees insisted on Mr. De Grasse's withdrawal. The most remarkable part of this transaction was, that when the students were assembled at meals, no one knew *which* was the colored student, Mr. D. having no visible traces of African descent.

THOMAS S. SYDNEY, the wit, the pure patriot, the almost self-taught scholar, cut off, alas! in the very bloom of his most promising youth.

SAMUEL RINGGOLD WARD, second cousin of Garnet, "the ablest thinker on his legs" which ANGLO-AFRICA has produced, whose powerful eloquence, brilliant repartee, and stubborn logic are as well known in England as in the United States.

The writer of this sketch has a school-boy remembrance of "Henry Garnet" of those days. In short, the recollections of this writer, and all the contemporary evidence he has been able to gather up from school-fellows yet surviving, picture out the school-boy Henry Garnet as quite the opposite of the nice, good, quiet little fellow, in whose mouth "butter would not melt."

He remained at school until 1828, when he made two voyages to Cuba in the capacity of cabin boy. In 1830 he again returned to the same school, for one year, during which year, the decided colonization views of the teacher, Mr. Charles C. Andrews, caused his removal by the Trustees, who were urged to dismiss him by the leading colored men of New York City. This was a sore trial for the "old scholars," whose attachment to their teacher was firm and ardent: it led to something of a struggle, in which the old heads of the people ultimately triumphed. The principal leaders in this movement were Henry Sipkins, an uncle to Thos. S. Sydney, William Hamilton, and that distinguished son of Virginia and of Accomac County, play-fellow of Hon. Henry A. Wise, Thomas Downing.

While yet a school-boy, and along with scores of his fellows, Henry fell into the ranks of the great celebration of the Abolition of Slavery in the State of New York, which was held July 5th, 1827. That was a celebration! A real, full-souled, full-voiced shouting for joy, and marching through the crowded streets, with feet jubilant to songs of freedom! It was a living proof of the poet's words—

> "Oh yield him back his privilege, no sea
> Swells like the bosom of a man set free."

First of all, Grand Marshal of the day was SAMUEL HARDENBURGH, a splendid-looking black man, in cocked hat and drawn sword, mounted on a milk-white steed; then his aids on horseback, dashing up and down the line; then the orator of the day, also mounted, with a handsome scroll, appearing like a *baton* in his right hand; then in due order, splendidly dressed in scarfs of silk with gold-edgings, and with colored bands of music, and their banners appropriately lettered and painted, followed, "THE NEW YORK AFRICAN SOCIETY FOR MUTUAL RELIEF," "THE WILBERFORCE BENEVOLENT SOCIETY," and "THE CLARKSON BENEVOLENT SOCIETY;"* then the people five or six abreast, from grown men to small boys. The side-walks were crowded with the wives, daughters, sisters, and mothers of the celebrants, representing every State in the Union, and not a few with gay bandanna handkerchiefs, betraying their West Indian birth: neither was Africa itself unrepresented, hundreds who had survived the middle passage, and a youth in slavery joined in the joyful procession. The people of those days rejoiced in their nationality, and hesitated not to call each other " Africans," or " descendants of Africa;" it was in after years, when they set up their just protest against the American Colonization Society and its principles that the term "African" fell into disuse and finally discredit. It was a proud day in the City of New York for our people, that 5th day of July, 1827. It was a proud day for Samuel Hardenburgh, Grand Marshal, splendidly mounted, as he passed through the west gate of the Park, saluted

---

* Of these societies, the sole survivor is "THE NEW YORK AFRICAN SOCIETY FOR MUTUAL RELIEF," which, in its fifty-sixth year, still holds a fine piece of real estate, and ministers, as of old, to its sick members.

the Mayor on the City Hall steps, and then took his way down Broadway to the Battery, &c. It was a proud day for his Aids, in their dress and trappings; it was a proud day for the Societies and their officers; it was a proud day, never to be forgotten by young lads, who, like Henry Garnet, first felt themselves impelled along that grand procession of liberty, which through perils oft, and dangers oft, through the gloom of midnight, dark and seemingly hopeless, dark and seemingly rayless, but now, through God's blessing, opening up to the joyful light of day, is still "*marching on.*"

## YOUTH.

These glorious dreams of Liberty, in 1827, were rudely dissipated two years after.

In 1829, when Henry was but fourteen years old, he went as cook and steward on board a schooner from New York to Alexandria and Washington, D. C. On his return home he was met at the wharf and told that the slave-hunters had found out and invaded the retreat of his family. His father, in escaping from them had leaped from the roof of the two-story house, No. 137 Leonard, two doors east of Centre Street; his mother had barely eluded their grasp. His sister had been arrested, tried as a "fugitive from labor," before Richard Riker, Recorder of the City of New York, and escaped by proving an "alibi," which in this case meant that she proved a residence in the city of New York at the very time when the witnesses for the prosecution swore that she was in Maryland a slave. His mother was kindly received and cared for by Mrs. and Mr. Sherlock, grocers, on the adjacent corner. Those excellent friends of the family are still living in the same place. The entire household furniture of the family was destroyed or stolen; and they were obliged to start anew in life, empty-handed. This news fell like a clap of thunder upon the young sea-farer; the first shock over, he was roused almost to madness. With the little money he had he purchased a large clasp-knife, openly carried it in his hand and sturdily marched up Broadway, waiting and hoping for the assault of the men-hunters. His mother was the very centre of all his hopes and affections, he cherished her with the most tender love and would gladly have forfeited his life rather than let any ill befal her. His friends found him, and hurried him out of the city, and sent him next day to the house of

4

Thomas Willis, at Jericho, L. I. At the house of this minister of the Society of Friends he met ELIAS HICKS and ANNA BRATHWAIT.

In 1829 he went to Smithtown, L. I., where he was bound to Captain Epenetus Smith. Here he remained two years, at the end of which period he lost the use of his right leg from an injury. In the same year his indentures were cancelled, and he returned to New York, where he rejoined his family.

This raid upon his peaceful family made a powerful impression on Henry. It seared his soul with an undying hatred of slavery, and touched his lips with that anti-slavery fervor and eloquence which has never gone out. Such onslaughts on colored families were not unfrequent at that time: no colored man's home was secure against them. They were not strictly popular, and the cases which came before Recorder Riker, of pleasant memory, found one who genially squinted towards the liberty of the captive, and who was a friend to the colored people generally.*

These slave hunts were not very frequent in New York City. Still they would occur, and, as the whole colored population were more or less either directly from the South, or linked by ties of marriage or consanguinity with their Southern brethren, a majority of whom had escaped from slavery, it is easy to see that the condition of these people was one of constant apprehension and jeopardy. The savings of long years of industry and economy, perhaps the little homes purchased as a shelter for old age, were ruthlessly swept away by the approach of the slave-hunter, even if, as was often the case, the alarm was false. This converted our free northern cities into slave-hunting grounds; steady and persistent industry of the colored people was frequently interrupted, and at any moment they might be forced to fly and "begin life anew."

One of the reasons for the relative poverty of the free colored people

---

* SMART DRAYTON, of Charleston, a colored man of great muscular power and pugilistic skill, was on a certain Fourth of July, assaulted in the Park by a gang of rowdies; placing his back against a tree, he whipped the crowd, and, *of course*, was arrested, and next morning brought up before the Recorder for assault and battery. One after another the dozen or twenty bruised and maimed individuals entered their complaints, when about one-third through the magistrate asked of the rest, "Do you complain against this man?" "And you?" "And you?" and getting an affirmative answer, exclaimed, "Begone, all of you; what a miserable set, to attack one man and be whipped!" "Drayton, you are discharged."

is hereby furnished. "PEACEFULLY" to pursue their various avocations for a livelihood, is an indispensable requisite for the advancement of any industrious, laboring people. How could we amass wealth, or even a small competency, when liable to such frequent and fatal interruptions to our lawful pursuits?

It may be asked by many, why the fugitives did not disperse throughout the country rather than crowd into the cities. There were two reasons why they did not. First, the free schools in the city formed an attraction which the freedman of that day esteemed as well as the freedman of to-day. So deeply did they feel the want of education in themselves, that they would run all risks, make any sacrifice to secure it. School privileges for colored children did not exist in the rural districts, with trifling exceptions; and the brutal ignorance in which, to an almost universal extent, New York and the adjoining States allowed colored boys and girls to grow up is a blot which will ever disfigure their fair fame. Nay, adding a meanness which approaches atrocity, they tax the hard earnings of the colored man to support schools and build schoolhouses for white children, from the doors of which the poor black youth are rudely driven.

Another reason was, that the country was no safer, if as safe, against kidnappers than the cities. In the ten years which elapsed between the passage of the Act of Emancipation, and the completion thereof, the slaveholders and their friends sold out of this State twenty per cent. of the colored population into slavery; the profits of this trade stimulated the dealers long after slavery had ceased, and there went prowling about the State, in one-horse buggies, or in sloops on the rivers, wretches in abundance who would snatch up a colored child and run down to Virginia and make a handsome sum by the operation. Nor were these operations confined to children; men would be coaxed away from home on various pretences and as suddenly transferred to the Slave States. The history of Solomon Northrop shows that this heinous practice was still kept up at a very recent date. In fact, slave-stealing can only end with slavery itself: destroy the market, and you destroy the trader.

It would seem therefore that, according to the lights before them, our people acted not unwisely in adhering to the cities.

In 1831, Henry H. Garnet entered the high-school for colored youth, newly organized in New York by Messrs. Curtis and Leiboldt; and hav-

ing a sound basis of the common branches of education, commenced the
study of Greek and Latin languages. To-day, with Oberlin, Allegheny
Institute, the High-School for Colored Youth in Philadelphia, with the
New England schools and colleges, all invitingly open to colored youth,
we can form no adequate estimate of the expanse of mind which young
Garnet and his fellows felt in having the classics opened to their greedy
intellects. Even colored men, of admitted force of character, were op-
posed to this innovation. Up to the opening of Mr. Andrews' school,
the education of the black man was considered complete by his white
friends when he reached the sentence of the PRIMERS of those days
which began with "No MAN.—" Further instruction then ceased, his
education was complete, he graduated, truly—"NO MAN." In the year
1831, when a couple of colored boys, admitted through the magnanimity of the teacher, carried away all the prizes of a collegiate Academy in
New York, the late COL. STONE, the far-famed and not illiberal editor
of the Commercial Advertiser, exclaimed, "These lads have done very
well, but—*cui bono?* What possible good can a classical education yield
them? Will we feel any better because the man who waits on our table
can read Virgil and Horace?"

But on the other hand, were some leading colored men who thought
differently. Among these were the REV. PETER WILLIAMS, Rector of
St. Philip's Church, Rev. Samuel E. Cornish, Mr. R. P. G. Wright,
of Schenectady, the revered father of the Rev. Theodore S. Wright, the
Rev. Theodore S. Wright himself, and others of kindred zeal. They
reasonably held that the vaunted superiority of the whites depended on
their superior education, and determined, by giving colored boys a thorough education to place them on a level with their white peers in this
regard at least. With the spread of Abolitionism these views gained
ground until the facilities for obtaining the higher branches of learning
are nearly as great for colored as for white youth.

Whilst pursuing his classical studies, in 1833, our student became
attached to the Sunday-school of the First Colored Presbyterian Church,
corner of William and Frankfort Streets, New York.* Here he had the

---

* This church edifice was more than a hundred years old. As a mark of progress,
or "poetic justice," it is worth relating that up to the early part of the present century, the old Dutch dames, who worshiped therein would require their slavo-girls
to carry their foot-stoves to the church, and there to remain outside during service,
on the grounds *that the blacks had no souls to be saved!*

good fortune to attract the attention and secure the warm interest of the
beloved THEODORE SEDGWICK WRIGHT, pastor of the church. This
devout man of God, ever in the service of his Divine Master, the Lord
and Saviour Jesus Christ, of humble yet unyielding faith, full of the
Holy Ghost, both as a preacher and a doer of the word, always interested, in season and out of season, in the religious state of his friends
and parishioners, whose kindly voice would break in upon, no matter
what discussion, with the inquiry, "Brother, do you enjoy religion?"
"Do you love Jesus Christ?" An abolitionist of the purest water and
most devoted zeal, this worthy minister cherished a warm interest in the
necessity for educating to the fullest extent capable colored youth as a
means of elevating his people. From the moment of seeing young Garnet, he selected him as one who should be educated. Subordinating all
other attainments to the "one thing needful," he first addressed himself to the religious culture of his young friend, whom he soon had the
consolation of calling his "son in the gospel." He then encouraged
him to prepare himself for the holy ministry, and towards that end ren-
dered him every assistance in his power. As David loved Jonathan, so
this father in Israel knit to his son in the Lord Jesus. In Garnet's
youth, now budding into manhood, and in the maturer years that followed, they were, allowing for the more brilliant gifts of the younger,
one in spirit, one in effort, one in all their noble resistances to caste and
slavery, one in their manifold and ceaseless endeavors to elevate the people of color, asserting together their native, noble manhood, in the teeth
of all comers from the slave-holder crowned with horrors to the pseudo-
abolitionist frightened at his shadow ; they were one in life, and scarcely
parted with the death of WRIGHT, whose mantle naturally fell upon the
shoulders of the loving survivor. On the one hand, the Rev. Mr.
Wright baptized Garnet, received him into his church, married him,
and was his life-long friend. On the other, Garnet, though borne down
with grief, preached the funeral sermon of his friend and benefactor, succeeded him, after a little time as pastor of his congregation, wrote his
epitaph, and assisted the bereaved members of the congregation in erect-
ing a fine monument in memory of him in the Union Cemetery.

Under such auspices, in 1835, he went to Canaan Academy, at Canaan,
New Hampshire, Rev. William Seales, principal ; he was kindly received
into the family of George Kimball, Esq. There he first met with Miss

Julia Williams, formerly a pupil of Miss Prudence Crandall, Canterbury, Connecticut, who was imprisoned for teaching colored girls: Miss Williams subsequently became his wife. Among the pupils at the Academy were his old schoolmates, Alexander Crummell and Thomas S. Sydney. They joyfully entered upon their studies, penetrated with the hopes of a race to whom the higher branches of human learning had hitherto been a sealed book.

But the spirit of caste, which we have already spoken of, as being, in the rural districts, still stronger against the education of colored youth than in the cities, soon concentrated its malign influence upon this Academy.

In August of the same year (1835) a mob assembled in Canaan, and with the aid of ninety-five yoke of oxen and two days' hard labor, finally succeeded in removing the Academy from its site and afterwards they destroyed it by fire. The same mob surrounded the house of Mr. Kimball and fired shot into the room occupied by Garnet: to add to the mean atrocity of the act, he was at that time, in consequence of increasing lameness, obliged to use a crutch in walking, and was confined to his room by a fever. But neither sickness, nor infirmity, nor the howling of the mob could subdue his fiery spirit; he spent most of the day in casting bullets in anticipation of the attack, and when the mob finally came he replied to their fire with a double-barrelled shot-gun, blazing from his window, and soon drove the cowards away.

In a short time after the destruction of the Academy, the pupils were compelled to leave the town. On the day of their departure some riotous persons fired a salute of many guns; the first was fired when the carriage in which they were riding was passing the mouth of the cannon. The three (Garnet, Crummell, and Sydney,) took stage at Hanover, N. H. Garnet, ill as he was, traveled day and night on the top of the stage-coach to Albany, N. Y., thus passing over the Granite Hills, and along the Green Mountains, (consecrated, in song, to Liberty,) across the valley of the Connecticut River, to that of the Hudson. At Albany they were taken in and lodged by the venerable Mrs. Johnson, mother of Mrs. Stephen Myers.

Garnet was, by this time, too sick to sit up. He was carried on board a steamboat and laid upon the forward deck, the only place where colored persons were "allowed" in those days. There was no awning, no shel-

ter from the broiling sun, no settee, no chair. His companions spread
their coats for a bed for him, and shaded his face with an umbrella; they
reached New York at nine o'clock in the evening, and he reached his
welcome home and bed, to which he was confined nearly two months.

In 1836, in company with his old fellow-students, he entered Oneida
Institute, then under the Presidency of that great reformer and scholar,
Rev. Beriah Green. Here, at length, the young seekers after knowledge,
found rest for their feet, not only in a region comparatively free from
caste-hate, but under the repose, the intellectual calm, of one of the
ablest thinkers of the century, whose most reticent modesty of habit
and severe plainness of living cannot hide the fact that he is the

> "bearer of the quiver
> Whose sun-like shafts pierce tempest-winged Error
> As light may pierce the clouds when they dissever
> In the calm regions of the orient day!"

It was worth while that these young men should have been expelled
from Canaan, in order to reach the atmosphere which Beriah Green had
made around Whitesboro, and that they might have the priceless privilege of learning, or rather sitting at his feet. To Crummell the opportunity was priceless in affording him that severe habit of thought which
has made him also an able and effective thinker; to Sydney it was an
intellectual training which developed his keen intelligence and wonderful
fidelity to the truthful in his own convictions; to Garnet as sobering
down that brilliant and difficultly curbed imagination, by the steady drill
of severer thought. There was no such thing, however, as curbing
Garnet's wit; it would occasionally break out, when somebody would
pretty surely "come to grief;" as in the following instance :—

On one occasion, when he was taking part in a colloquy, at the exhibition of the junior class, a reckless, pro-slavery young man, named
Cills, one of the audience, had armed himself with a large pumpkin; at
a favorable moment he aimed it at Garnet, throwing it with full force
from the gallery; missing its aim, it was dashed in pieces on the
stage, many fragments flying in the faces of the ladies below. In the
midst of the great excitement which followed, Garnet quietly stepped
forward, and looking gravely on some of the smashed pieces, quietly
said, "My good friends, do not be alarmed, it is only a soft pumpkin;
some gentleman has thrown away his head, and lo! his brains are dashed

out!'' From that day forward, the young man was called "*Pumpkin Head Cills.*" *

And so the golden academic days of their golden youth, glided by, and these young men, well knit to each other through kindred perils, and kindred forecast of the struggle for rights to which the providence of the Almighty had ordained them, went forth into the world with minds and hearts most happily trained for the labors allotted to them. If they were not so well "up" in Greek, Latin, and Mathematics, as the graduates of Harvard and Yale, they were more thoroughly masters of the philosophy of reform, and were profoundly taught in those great moral principles, the direct and legitimate outgrowth of the Bible, which stood them in better stead in the path through which they were destined to tread.

## MANHOOD.

Returning to New York City in 1840, Mr. Garnet delivered his maiden speech at the annual meeting of the American Anti-Slavery Society in May of that year. It was a fine effort, full of the promise of that surpassing eloquence, wit and pathos which has distinguished his subsequent career. Such at least is the opinion of those who listened to what they call *the* speech of that anniversary. We sincerely regret that the most careful search has failed to procure a copy of this speech, from which it would have been a pleasure and a profit to the reader to make copious extracts for these pages.

In September, 1840, he graduated with honors at Oneida Institute, and settled at Troy, N. Y., where he taught the colored district school, and conducted religious meetings in the old lecture room of the First Presbyterian Church which had been purchased by the colored Presbyterians with the view of organizing a church.

He was ordained a ruling elder in 1841, at the time of the organization of the church. In the same year he was united in the bonds of a most happy wedlock, to Miss Julia Williams. Having, in the interim,

* On another occasion when at Utica, he was dragged out of one car by four men, and thrust into another where he was compelled to sit alone: he put his head out of the window, and said to his assailants, who were puffing and blowing, "Gentlemen, you are quite correct in supposing that I have sufficient dignity to fill an entire car."

studied theology under the direction of the Rev. Dr. Beman, he was in 1842 licensed to preach, by the Presbytery of Troy. In that year seventy members were added to the church. In 1843 he was ordained, and installed first pastor of the Liberty Street Presbyterian Church in Troy. This post he held until 1848, a period of nearly ten years of his ministry. Apart from the physical suffering caused by the amputation of the diseased limb in 1840, this was, perhaps, the most marked period of his useful life.

Under him, the beloved pastor, rapidly grew a large, pious, and devoted people, foremost in every good work, self-elevating, self-improving, self-advancing, so that they became as a light upon the hill-side, towards which their brethren in other cities, and their friends of the other class of citizens, might look, and point with pleasure, as a proof of the vincibility of all mere human distinctions, by rightly-directed human endeavor.

As a proof of the esteem in which he was held by the whites, he was elected a life-member of the Young Men's Literary Society of Troy, and acceptably took a prominent part in their various discussions.

In 1839–40 he published, at Troy, a weekly paper characteristically named the "CLARION," throwing out in type the bugle notes wherewith he was wont by voice and mien to lead the people to battle against their surrounding, almost overwhelming, oppressions.

Besides his local labors as the efficient pastor of his beloved congregation, there was no good work, or progressive movement relating to " our people," in which he was not found in the foremost rank. As an ardent advocate of the Temperance movement, he was always one of the selected speakers in the great annual gatherings at some town on the Hudson, where a gathering of thousands of our people, generally under the lead of MR. STEPHEN MYERS, met, formed a procession, and then, in some pleasant, shady grove listened to the eloquence of our foremost men.

A firm and zealous advocate of the Liberty Party, he was one of the standard bearers of that organization, and the most successful speech that ever fell from his lips was delivered at the Liberty Party Convention held in Buffalo in 1843: we must again repeat our regret at being unable to procure a copy from which to make extracts.

From 1836 until 1850, the colored citizens of the State of New York were in the habit of holding annual conventions in Albany or one of the

5

provincial cities for the purpose of devising means for their advancement, the principal of which was an earnest endeavor to secure the right to vote on the same basis with the whites. These meetings answered a double purpose: they knit together the oppressed living in all parts of the State, enabled them to cheer and encourage each other in the up-hill road in which it was their destiny to tread; they also afforded to the dominant (white) class an opportunity to witness the fine talent for business and oratory which these conventions always exhibited. The day sessions were devoted to business, and the evening sessions to speaking *at* and *to* the crowded audiences of the whites whose convictions were thus reached by evidence which could not be gainsayed. Foremost among the leaders of these conventions were the Revs. Theodore S. Wright, Henry H. Garnet, Samuel Ward, Charles B. Ray, Messrs. Stephen Myers, William H. Topp, Francis Thompson, William Rich and others. There were good times at most of them, there being just enough difference of opinion to produce lively debates without the bitter remembrances which sometimes remain after similar gatherings. Each session was opened and closed with prayer; there was a feeling of nearness to God, and dependence on his help, and submission to his Divine providence and will, which it is pleasant to look back upon, in these days, when even a colored national convention—intellectual at that— overlooking the concrete living God, is content to appeal to one of his supposed abstract attributes.

The New York City riots of 1863, among other disasters, has caused the destruction of nearly all the printed minutes of these conventions— our Alexandrine Library—from which some of the noblest pages in the history of our people could have been selected. We have, thus far, been able to find only the "Minutes of the Fifth Annual Convention of the Colored Citizens of the State of New York, held in the City of Schenectady on the 18th, 19th, and 20th September, 1844."

From this, as illustrative of the time, and of the subject of this sketch twenty years ago, we make several extracts exhibiting the great leader, and to what labors he urged the people, and also the spirit of his devoted friend and coadjutor.

## "CALL FOR THE CONVENTION."

"FELLOW CITIZENS OF NEW YORK:—

"You are invited to attend the Annual Convention of the colored citizens of this state, and our friends, which will convene by leave of Divine Providence in the city of Schenectady, on Wednesday, September 18, at 10 A. M.

Your Committee believe that the success which has attended our former Conventions will be sufficient to secure a large attendance to the one anticipated.

In accordance with a resolution which was passed at the Rochester Convention, the delegates to the approaching meeting are requested to bring with them the religious, educational, property and Society Statistics of the districts which they represent.

It is the opinion of the laborious and long suffering among us, that our sphere of action should be enlarged:—that while we continue with unabated zeal to knock at the door of the Capitol until we obtain equal suffrage, at the same time we should consider every department of reform that is interesting to men, and that promises to improve our moral and intellectual being.

Brethren, we expect a great meeting. We know what to expect from New Yorkers. From that auspicious day when our State Banner was first flung to the breeze, to our last great gathering at Rochester, we have not failed in a single Convention. We have withstood every opposition with unflinching perseverance, although we have been assailed by foes from abroad, and enemies in our midst. But now the tide begins to turn, and smiling hope with anchor sure and steadfast, points to certain victory.

We invite our fellow-citizens in every part of the State to make a grand rally. Come from the regions of the lakes and the broad valleys of the west. Come from your mountain homes of the east—the rocky ramparts of the North, from the sea-beaten shores of the South. Come, hoary-headed sires, we desire your counsel. Come, young men, and unite your strength, and form a nucleus of Liberty around which the moral strength of the whole State shall gather. We need and earnestly solicit the aid and approbation of our noble-hearted women, who have never been backward in any measure of general good.—A brighter day is dawning—success is now certain, for God is with us. He speaks from his throne—"Blow ye the trumpet in the land—cry, gather together, and say, assemble yourselves." Then—

"Prayer strengthened for the trial come together,
Put on the harness for the moral fight,
And with the blessings of our Heavenly Father
MAINTAIN THE RIGHT."

H. H. GARNET,
Ch'n of Central Com.
WM. RICH,
WM. P. McINTYRE,
C. S. MORTON,
RICH'D THOMPSON, JR.,
J. WANDELL,
F. THOMPSON.

"P. S. The Committee have consulted the people of Schenectady, and it is their desire that the Convention should be held at the time announced in the Call. This desire was urged in consequence of some local circumstances altogether beyond their control, and intimately connected with the usefulness of the Convention.

H. H. G.

TROY, JUNE 16, 1844.

2nd. We present the

## REPORT,

*On the best Means for the promotion of the Enfranchisement of our people.*

The committee have been brief in their report, so that its length might not be an objection to its perusal.

A resort to no one class of means could remove the disabilities which obstruct our improvement, but it requires a happy combination of all laudable pursuits to secure such an end. Yet there are some particular pursuits which would tend more than others to remove the prejudice which a majority of our fellow-citizens cherish towards us. We proceed to name some of the most prominent and available.

1. A general diffusion of literary, scientific and religious knowledge among the people. This can be done, as it has already been done in some places, by the establishment of Public Libraries, Lyceums, and Public Lectures.

2. By the careful education of our youth, and holding out to them additional encouragement, in proportion to the extra difficulties which they have to encounter.

3. By giving our children useful trades, and by patronizing those who may have engaged in useful handicrafts.

4. The committee would urge as first in importance the removal of our people from the cities and large towns, and the betaking of themselves to the country. Prejudice is so strong in cities, and custom is so set and determined, that it is impossible for us to emerge from the most laborious and the least profitable occupations.

For instance, in the city of New York, a colored citizen cannot obtain a license to drive a cart! Many such like inconveniences beset them on every hand. Thus scores of men, whose intelligence (we would say nothing of their enterprise) is sufficient to entitle them to stations of trust and profit, are compelled to drudge out their lives for a scanty subsistence. It has been seen, that when they have satisfied the demands of the landlord, provided their fuel, and have paid devotion to the shrine of fashion, there is nothing left for "a rainy day," and they often die in want.

Not so in the country, where every man is known, and even our people who are so much abused in cities are respected almost according to their moral worth. The committee would not say that there are none of these difficulties in the country—but that there are far less than are met with in cities, we do affirm.

In the country, no man is prohibited from driving a cart! Nay, he can raise his own horses and cattle, and drive them over his fruitful fields, or to the fair, or to the market, or elsewhere. He can go to the woods and get his fuel, and burn the same in his log cabin. when winter winds are abroad, without fearing lest his solid comfort should be interrupted by a surly landlord, who is as certain to come every three months, as death is at the end of life.

In the towns of Syracuse and Geneva, among a colored population of some eight hundred, there are more voters according to the odious $250 qualification, than there are in New York city, which has eighteen or twenty thousand colored inhabitants.

Whoever will take the pains to examine facts on the subject, will find that real influence and property dwindles away in the hands of our people, as we approach cities and large towns. In New York City there is but one * instance among our High Schools, Theological Seminaries, and Colleges, in which a colored youth can avail himself of its benefits. In many other cities not even one exception is found.

Indeed, the Committee know of no College or Female Seminary in any city of the Union whose doors are open for our children.

If the talents of our young men, which in the cities are hindered in their growth were transplanted to the country, there is no prejudice so strong as to be able to roll back the tide of our enfranchisement.†

In every prosperous country, and among every powerful and influential people, whose territory would admit of the employment, agriculture has contributed its full share of wealth and glory. In our country, where labor is honorable, and where the fruitful earth invites the husbandman to dress and till it, agriculture is emphatically the surest road to temporal happiness.

In the proudest days of Rome, when she stretched out her sceptre over a subjugated world, she called her favorite from the furrowed field. Her legislators encouraged her farmers, nor did the sun of her glory begin to set, until her fields were neglected, and her sons exchanged that honorable labor for the luxury and licentiousness of cities and camps. The Committee would venture to say, that if agriculture bore such an important part in promoting the greatness of an entire nation, the same course would secure an influence for the oppressed portion of any people.

But every man that removes to the country, or to some small and growing town, need not necessarily become a farmer. If he be a mechanic, he may turn his attention to his trade, with great advantage. Cities are not in themselves unfavorable to our people, but public opinion in them is such as to render it next to impossible for us to rise above

* Union Theological Seminary.

† A member of the committee was a short time ago informed by the esteemed Governor of Massachusetts, that there is a humble, though upright colored citizen of his town, who is doing more by his example and intelligence to benefit his people, than all other human efforts. He would not have been noticed in a large city.

dependence. Let our men become the owners of the soil, and they shall be the founders of towns and villages; and as they grow up, they may grow with them, and may give tone and character to a just and liberal public sentiment.

Let a few families select a good spot, having favorable water privileges, and other advantages—let them subdue the forests, erect their mills, and build their workshops, and in a few years they will have a thriving village. Or let them go to some youthful towns just springing into existence.

In conclusion the Committee would advise families and individuals to leave the large cities, and repair to the country, and by observing the other recommendations in the report, they will use the best and most certain means to promote our happiness and enfranchisement.

Signed,        H. H. GARNET.

3rd. We cannot resist adding here the letter of Rev. T. S. Wright, addressed to the same convention, showing the spirit which actuated the warmest friend, admirer and supporter of the Rev. Mr. Garnet, for "a man may be known by the company he keeps."

New York, Sept. 17, 1844.

*To the President of the State Convention, convened at Schenectady, on the 18th inst.*

The subscriber through you, sir, begs the privilege to state, that having, in connection with others, the responsibility imposed upon him of representing the city of New York, in your honorable and important convocation, deeply regrets that in consequence of severe indisposition, he is denied the anticipated happiness of discharging that responsibility, by participating in your intrinsically important deliberations.

This circumstance, unimportant in others, and to the noble cause for the promotion of which you are convened, causes anxiety to myself, that my brethren of the city of my earliest and some of my most pleasant recollections and associations, may be apprised of the cause of my absence; and further, that the noble, the disinterested band of patriots and reformers, gathered from every section of our great, though to our people, unjust state, with whom it has been my high privilege and honor to labor and pray at previous conventions, may rest assured that my love for the great principles which brought into existence this great conventional movement has in no wise abated, nor has my zeal, in their propagations, nor my confidence under God of their final and glorious triumph.

If God be just and true, his immutable and eternal truth will ultimately annihilate that cruel prejudice, injustice and oppression, which in our state has plundered our franchise, or fundamental rights, and with a cruel, bloody and wicked hand now crushes millions in this nation to the dust.

May I not hope for your forbearance whilst I express my great solicitude, that this convention, like those which have preceded it guided by the Spirit from on high in all its decisions may lean on God; planting itself on the great fundamental principles of his eternal and immutable truth, not on worldly expediency or on time-serving policy? The present is a period of danger. The political tornado is now sweeping through the land. And it cannot be expected that we in common with the multitude should be affected more or less, by the miserable sophisms wielded by many of both of the two great political parties, to carry the nation. My confidence is in the principles upon which the Liberty party is based. I believe they are just. But were it my happiness to be a member of the convention, I would not be anxious for its formal identification with this party. I should not advocate it, unless an issue between this and one of the other parties were forced upon me, or some action was proposed to the disparagement of the Liberty party. I would then feel religiously called upon to stand by liberty principles. If I was alone enjoying the sweet consciousness of having the truth with me, and the approbation of the God of the oppressed before whom as I am emphatically reminded I may be summoned to appear, before the return of another annual convention, having had, during the hours of my recent affliction, time for deliberate, solemn reflection on this subject with its bearings upon the nominally free and upon the more forlorn condition of our brethren in bonds, in humility I would say to my brethren of the delegation, if I were pronouncing my last dying words, adhere to these principles, swerve neither to the right nor the left, they are in my humble judgment truth indestructible and God-given.

Fear not results, leave them with God. He will take care of his own truth.

May the guidance and blessing of the Spirit from on high, the spirit of wisdom, be upon the delegation. Amen.

THEODORE SEDGWICK WRIGHT.

The Chairman having announced that there was no more business claiming the attention of the convention,

On motion, the following resolutions were adopted:

*Resolved*, That this convention return their thanks to the Trustees of the 1st Baptist Church of Schenectady, for their kindness in granting the free use of their house of worship.

*Resolved*, That we return our thanks to our colored friends in Schenectady for their hospitality during our stay in this city.

*Resolved*, That we shall remember with gratitude the kindness of the citizens generally, during the sessions of this convention.

Resolutions were also adopted, thanking the sexton of the Church, the Vice Presidents, the Secretaries, and Business Committees of the convention, and one of thanks to the central committee. The Rev. H. H. Garnet then led the convention in devout thanks to Almighty God. After singing a hymn of praise, the convention adjourned.

We gladly reprint this letter of the Rev. Mr. Wright's, more for the benefit of the future than the present; "For this bright luminary has not so far sunk into the twilight of past years, but its radiance still cheers and warms the horizon it has left."*

Comparing the proceedings of the State Convention at Schenectady in 1844 with those of the National Convention held in Syracuse in 1865, there is a singular sameness in the Resolutions, and the recommendations, and general proceedings, with two marked exceptions: the earlier convention devoutly followed what a poet has recently so well expressed—

——"Cast all your cares on God,
That anchor holds——"

the other difference is in their financial arrangements; the elder convention placing no pecuniary burden upon those who might elect or be elected to its succeeding annual gathering.

From the conventions of that date, the memory naturally glides to another "institution," hardly less remarkable, or of less influence in the city of New York—UNION HALL, the great meeting room, the *agora*, the *forum* of the people and their leaders,—a Tammany Hall, except

* Earl Russell on Sir Robert Peel.

that it was not the property of a party, nor the minion of slavery, nor the tippling room of the "great unwashed." Under the old Broadway Tabernacle, occupying nearly one-half its basement story, a space of fifty feet by one hundred, broken into by huge round brick columns, which supported the floor above; dimly lighted by a half dozen camphene lamps badly trimmed, the floor nearly covered by movable benches, a dilapidated platform with a slightly elevated seat for the Chairman—such was the appearance of UNION HALL. Its keeper, Mr. WILLIAM P. JOHNSON, an elder in the First Colored Presbyterian Church, was heart and soul devoted to the elevation of his brethren, whether free or in bonds. A more devoted servant of God, a more earnest and diligent worker for the elevation of our people, it has not been our fortune to meet. It was fortunate for our people that this good man held, for their convenience, this meeting-place, which he let to them at a low price, often not paying for lights, for any good public movement, whether temperance, social reform, the franchise. Gerrit Smith's land, anti-colonization, the rebuke or praise of Governors or Congressmen—not forgetting "the old man eloquent"—or whatever matter the colored citizens of New York felt called upon to discuss in "Mass Meeting."

And certainly, the practice afforded in the varied discussions in Union Hall, has not failed to bring out men and measures, which have been felt on almost every part of the Union, in Great Britain and its dependencies, and even in Africa. If anything could prove that every effort, even in the part of the humblest, if made in the right spirit and in the right direction, must succeed in doing good, then the history of Union Hall and its meetings will do so. Free speech, untrammeled by party considerations, or political rewards, reached into the very marrow of things, and men became accustomed to handle questions on their real merits, and were wont to be moved, and accustomed to move others by motives based upon real truths. Hence, among the graduates, if we may so term them, of Union Hall, there went forth men accustomed to think and act. Among a few that may be named here, are Newport Henry, Jacob Francis, Philip A. Bell and J. Holland Townsend, who went to California to succeed in digging for rights rather than gold, and have made their mark on the statute-book of the Golden State by causing the abolition of its worst pro-slavery laws; William P. Powell, whose five years' residence in Liverpool, winning his way up to a very important appointment under the crown, elevated the character of our people in that most pro-slavery of English cities; Henry J. Johnson, now become a successful lawyer in Liberia; George T. Downing, whose long-continued and masterly efforts to secure equal school privileges in Rhode Island have made him a power, held in awe by the time-serving caste-cursed legislators of that State, and HENRY HIGHLAND GARNET, who has preached in the Capitol of the nation, the noble representative of our race.

For, although living in Troy, Mr. Garnet would occasionally swoop down on Union Hall, and carry all before him. Perhaps his finest feat in this direction occurred in connection with the very convention named above, held at Schenectady. It was during the best days of the Liberty party, and the Colored State Convention held in Rochester the year before (1843), called especially with relation to the franchise, had passed a resolution endorsing the said party. Some of the New Yorkers, at a meeting held at Union Hall, adopted a protest against this resolution, and instructed their delegates to present the same to the Schenectady Convention. This they did, but after a severe discussion, the convention refused to accept the protest, or permit its appearance on the minutes. In this discussion, Mr. Garnett went with the convention. After the vote, the protesters resigned membership of the convention, returned to New York, and called a public meeting in Union Hall to hear their "report," which they had printed for the occasion.

The Hall was jammed; the "protesters" were in excellent spirits; they were "at home," and had a good case to lay before the people; they anticipated a large vote in favor of their report. After the usual skirmishing about Chairman, &c., in which they won, the report was in order, was read, and a motion for its adoption supported by a speech. The discussion took this form:

1. The "protesters" held that our people, seeking the franchise at the hands of all the parties in the State, as a right, had acted injudiciously, in allying themselves to any *one* party, thereby incurring the opposition of the others.

2. It was held by the other side that the "franchise" would not be worth the having from any party or parties, who denied the "patriotic colored citizens of New York the right of thinking as they please."

The discussion went on; at length the leader of "the protesters" delivered his set speech, in which, after indignantly proclaiming that "the right of petition "had been outraged by the myrmidons of the Liberty Party at Schenectady, he called on his fellow-citizens, &c., &c."

In an instant Garnet was up. His tall form seemed to dilate as with uplifted arm and flashing eye he exclaimed, "The eagle screams of liberty, why may not I?" Then followed a masterly argument, interspersed with so much wit, ridicule and sarcasm, and winding up with an appeal to the audience which carried them away with shouts and cheers.

The vote was taken and the protesters, dreadfully voted down, could not get the hang of things, the why and the wherefore for some time afterwards. Mr. Garnet has, on several occasions since then, invited one or more of these gentlemen to try conclusions with them on the platform, but they have not seen their way clear to accept. For one of them, we may add, we speak "by authority."

In 1843. at a National Convention of colored citizens, held at Buffalo. New York, Mr. Garnet offered for adoption his "ADDRESS TO THE SLAVES OF THE UNITED STATES."

# AN ADDRESS

To the Slaves of the United States of America, (REJECTED BY THE NATIONAL CONVENTION, HELD IN BUFFALO, N. Y., 1843), BY HENRY HIGHLAND GARNET.

BRETHREN AND FELLOW-CITIZENS:—Your brethren of the North, East, and West have been accustomed to meet together in National Conventions, to sympathize with each other, and to weep over your unhappy condition. In these meetings we have addressed all classes of the free, but we have never, until this time, sent a word of consolation and advice to you. We have been contented in sitting still and mourning over your sorrows, earnestly hoping that before this day your sacred liberties would have been restored. But, we have hoped in vain. Years have rolled on, and tens of thousands have been borne on streams of blood and tears, to the shores of eternity. While you have been oppressed, we have also been partakers with you; nor can we be free while you are enslaved. We, therefore, write to you as being bound with you.

Many of you are bound to us, not only by the ties of a common humanity, but we are connected by the more tender relations of parents, wives, husbands, children, brothers, and sisters, and friends. As such we most affectionately address you.

Slavery has fixed a deep gulf between you and us, and while it shuts out from you the relief and consolation which your friends would willingly render, it afflicts and persecutes you with a fierceness which we might not expect to see in the fiends of hell. But still the Almighty Father of mercies has left to us a glimmering ray of hope, which shines out like a lone star in a cloudy sky. Mankind are becoming wiser, and better—the oppressor's power is fading, and you, every day, are becoming better informed, and more numerous. Your grievances, brethren, are many. We shall not attempt, in this short address, to present to the world all the dark catalogue of this nation's sins, which have been committed upon an innocent people. Nor is it indeed necessary, for you feel them from day to day, and all the civilized world look upon them with amazement.

Two hundred and twenty-seven years ago, the first of our injured race were brought to the shores of America. They came not with glad spirits to select their homes in the New World. They came not with their own consent, to find an unmolested enjoyment of the blessings of this fruitful soil. The first dealings they had with men calling themselves Christians, exhibited to them the worst features of corrupt and sordid hearts: and convinced them that no cruelty is too great, no villainy and no robbery too abhorrent for even enlightened men to perform, when influenced by avarice and lust. Neither did they come flying upon the wings of Liberty, to a land of freedom. But they came with broken hearts, from their beloved native land, and were doomed to unrequited toil and deep degradation. Nor did the evil of their bondage end at their emancipation by death. Succeeding generations inherited their chains, and millions have come from eternity into time, and have returned again to the world of spirits, cursed and ruined by American slavery.

The propagators of the system, or their immediate ancestors, very soon discovered its growing evil, and its tremendous wickedness, and secret promises were made to destroy it. The gross inconsistency of a people holding slaves, who had themselves "ferried o'er the wave" for freedom's sake, was too apparent to be entirely overlooked. The voice of Freedom cried, "Emancipate your slaves." Humanity supplicated with tears for the deliverance of the children of Africa. Wisdom urged her solemn plea. The bleeding captive plead his innocence, and pointed to Christianity who stood weeping at the cross. Jehovah frowned upon the nefarious institution, and thunderbolts, red with vengeance, struggled to leap forth to blast the guilty wretches who maintained it. But all was vain. Slavery had stretched its dark wings of death over the land, the Church stood silently by—the priests prophesied falsely, and the people loved to have it so. Its throne is established, and now it reigns triumphant.

Nearly three millions of your fellow-citizens are prohibited by law and public opinion, (which in this country is stronger than law,) from reading the Book of Life. Your intellect has been destroyed as much as possible, and every ray of light they have attempted to shut out from your minds. The oppressors themselves have become involved in the ruin. They have become weak, sensual, and rapacious—they have cursed you—they have cursed themselves—they have cursed the earth which they have trod.

The colonists threw the blame upon England. They said that the mother country entailed the evil upon them, and that they would rid themselves of it if they could. The world thought they were sincere, and the philanthropic pitied them. But time soon tested their sincerity. In a few years the colonists grew strong, and severed themselves from the British Government. Their independence was declared, and they took their station among the sovereign powers of the earth. The declaration was a glorious document. Sages admired it, and the patriotic of every nation reverenced the God-like sentiments which it contained. When the power of Government returned to their hands, did they emancipate the slaves? No; they rather added new links to our chains. Were they ignorant of the principles of Liberty? Certainly they were not. The sentiments of their revolutionary orators fell in burning eloquence upon their hearts, and with one voice they cried, LIBERTY OR DEATH. Oh what a sentence was that! It ran from soul to soul like electric fire, and nerved the arm of thousands to fight in the holy cause of Freedom. Among the diversity of opinions that are entertained in regard to physical resistance, there are but a few found to gainsay that stern declaration. We are among those who do not.

SLAVERY! How much misery is comprehended in that single word. What mind is there that does not shrink from its direful effects? Unless the image of God be obliterated from the soul, all men cherish the love of Liberty. The nice discerning political economist does not regard the sacred right more than the untutored African who roams in the wilds of Congo. Nor has the one more right to the full enjoyment of his freedom than the other. In every man's mind the good seeds of liberty are planted. and he who brings his fellow down so low, as to make him contented with a condition of slavery, commits the highest crime against God and man. Brethren, your oppressors aim to do this. They endeavor to make you as much like brutes as possible. When they have blinded the eyes of your mind—when they have embittered the sweet waters of life—when they have shut out the light which shines from the word of God—then, and not till then, has American slavery done its perfect work.

To such Degradation it is sinful in the Extreme for you to make voluntary Submission. The divine commandments you are in duty bound to reverence and obey. If you do not obey them, you will surely meet with the displeasure of the Almighty. He requires you to love him supremely, and your neighbor as yourself—to keep the Sabbath day holy—to search the Scriptures—and bring up your children with respect for his laws, and to worship no other God but him. But slavery sets all these at nought, and hurls defiance in the face of Jehovah. The forlorn condition in which you are placed, does not destroy your moral obligation to God. You are not certain of heaven, because you suffer yourselves to remain in a state of slavery, where you cannot obey the commandments of the Sovereign of the universe. If the ignorance of slavery is a passport to heaven, then it is a blessing, and no curse, and you should rather desire its perpetuity than its abolition. God will not receive slavery, nor ignorance, nor any other state of mind, for love and obedience to him. Your condition does not absolve you from your moral obligation. The diabolical injustice by which your liberties are cloven down, neither God, nor angels, or just men, command you to suffer for a single moment. Therefore it is your solemn and imperative duty to use every means, both moral, intellectual, and physical, that promises success. If a band of heathen men should attempt to enslave a race of Christians, and to place their children under the influence of some false religion, surely, Heaven would frown upon the men who would not resist such aggression, even to death. If, on the other hand, a band of Christians should attempt to enslave a race of heathen men, and to curtail slavery upon them, and to keep them in heathenism in the midst of Christianity, the God of heaven would smile upon every effort which the injured might make to disenthral themselves.

Brethren, it is as wrong for your lordly oppressors to keep you in slavery, as it was for the man thief to steal our ancestors from the coast of Africa. You should therefore now use the same manner of resistance, as would have been just in our ancestors, when the bloody foot-prints of the first remorseless soul-thief was placed upon the shores of our father-land. The humblest peasant is as free in the sight of God as the proudest monarch that ever swayed a sceptre. Liberty is a spirit sent out from God, and like its great Author, is no respecter of persons.

Brethren, the time has come when you must act for yourselves. It is an old and true saying that, "if hereditary bondmen would be free, they must themselves strike the blow." You can plead your own cause, and do the work of emancipation better than any others. The nations of the old world are moving in the great cause of universal freedom, and some of them at least will, ere long, do you justice. The combined powers of Europe have placed their broad seal of disapprobation upon the African slave-trade. But in the slave-holding parts of the United States, the trade is as brisk as ever. They buy and sell you as though you were brute beasts. The North has done much—her opinion of slavery in the abstract is known. But in regard to the South, we adopt the opinion of the *New York Evangelist*—"We have advanced so far, that the cause apparently waits for a more effectual door to be thrown open than has been yet." We are about to point you to that more effectual door. Look around you, and behold the bosoms of your loving wives heaving with untold agonies! Hear the cries of your poor children! Remember the stripes your fathers bore. Think of the torture and disgrace of your noble mothers. Think of your wretched sisters, loving virtue and purity, as they are driven into concubinage and are exposed to the unbridled lusts of incarnate devils. Think of the undying glory that hangs around the ancient name of Africa :—and forget not that you are native-born American citizens, and as such, you are justly entitled to all the rights that are granted to the freest. Think how many tears you have poured out upon the soil which you have cultivated with unrequited toil and enriched with your blood; and then go to your lordly enslavers and tell them plainly, that you *are determined to be free*. Appeal to their sense of justice, and tell them that they have no more right to oppress you, than you have to enslave them. Entreat them to remove the grievous burdens which they have imposed upon you, and to remunerate you for your labor. Promise them renewed diligence in the cultivation of the soil, if they will render to you an equivalent for your services. Point them to the increase of happiness and prosperity in the British West-Indies since the Act of Emancipation. Tell them in language which they cannot misunderstand, of the exceeding sinfulness of slavery, and of a future judgment, and of the righteous retributions of an indignant God. Inform them that all you desire is FREEDOM, and that nothing else will suffice. Do this, and for ever after cease to toil for the heartless tyrants, who give you no other reward but stripes and abuse. If they then commence the work of death, they, and not you, will be responsible for the consequences. You had far better all die—*die immediately*, than live slaves, and entail your wretchedness upon your posterity. If you would be free in this generation, here is your only hope. However much you and all of us may desire it, there is not much hope of redemption without the shedding of blood. If you must bleed, let it all come at once—rather *die freemen, than live to be the slaves*. It is impossible, like the children of Israel, to make a grand exodus from the land of bondage. The Pharaohs are on both sides of the blood-red waters! You cannot move *en masse*, to the dominions of the British Queen—nor can you pass through Florida and overrun Texas, and at last find peace in Mexico. The propagators of American slavery are spending their blood and treasure, that they may plant the black flag in the heart of Mexico and riot in the halls of the Montezumas. In the language of the Rev. Robert Hall, when addressing the volunteers of Bristol, who were rushing forth to repel the invasion of Napoleon, who threatened to lay waste the fair homes of England, "Religion is too much interested in your behalf, not to shed over you her most gracious influences."

You will not be compelled to spend much time in order to become inured to hardships. From the first moment that you breathed the air of heaven, you have been accustomed to nothing else but hardships. The heroes of the American Revolution were never put upon harder fare than a peck of corn and a few herrings per week. You have not become enervated by the luxuries of life. Your sternest energies have been

7

beaten out upon the anvil of severe trial. Slavery has done this, to make you subservient to its own purposes; but it has done more than this, it has prepared you for any emergency. If you receive good treatment, it is what you could hardly expect; if you meet with pain, sorrow, and even death, these are the common lot of the slaves.

Fellow-men! patient sufferers! behold your dearest rights crushed to the earth! See your sons murdered, and your wives, mothers and sisters doomed to prostitution. In the name of the merciful God, and by all that life is worth, let it no longer be a debatable question, whether it is better to choose *Liberty* or *death*.

In 1822, Denmark Veazie, of South Carolina, formed a plan for the liberation of his fellow-men. In the whole history of human efforts to overthrow slavery, a more complicated and tremendous plan was never formed. He was betrayed by the treachery of his own people, and died a martyr to freedom. Many a brave hero fell, but history, faithful to her high trust, will transcribe his name on the same monument with Moses, Hampden, Tell, Bruce and Wallace, Toussaint L'Ouverture, Lafayette and Washington. That tremendous movement shook the whole empire of slavery. The guilty soul-thieves were overwhelmed with fear. It is a matter of fact, that at that time, and in consequence of the threatened revolution, the slave States talked strongly of emancipation. But they blew but one blast of the trumpet of freedom, and then laid it aside. As these men became quiet, the slaveholders ceased to talk about emancipation: and now behold your condition to-day! Angels sigh over it, and humanity has long since exhausted her tears in weeping on your account!

The patriotic Nathaniel Turner followed Denmark Veazie. He was goaded to desperation by wrong and injustice. By despotism, his name has been recorded on the list of infamy, and future generations will remember him among the noble and brave.

Next arose the immortal Joseph Cinque, the hero of the Amistad. He was a native African, and by the help of God he emancipated a whole ship-load of his fellow men on the high seas. And he now sings of liberty on the sunny hills of Africa and beneath his native palm-trees, where he hears the lion roar and feels himself as free as that king of the forest.

Next arose Madison Washington, that bright star of freedom, and took his station in the constellation of true heroism. He was a slave on board the brig Creole, of Richmond, bound to New Orleans, that great slave mart. with a hundred and four others. Nineteen struck for liberty or death. But one life was taken, and the whole were emancipated, and the vessel was carried into Nassau, New Providence.

Noble men! Those who have fallen in freedom's conflict. their memories will be cherished by the true-hearted and the God-fearing in all future generations; those who are living, their names are surrounded by a halo of glory.

Brethren, arise, arise! Strike for your lives and liberties. Now is the day and the hour. Let every slave throughout the land do this, and the days of slavery are numbered. You cannot be more oppressed than you have been—you cannot suffer greater cruelties than you have already. *Rather die freemen than live to be slaves.* Remember that you are FOUR MILLIONS!

It is in your power so to torment the God-cursed slaveholders, that they will be glad to let you go free. If the scale was turned. and black men were the masters and white men the slaves, every destructive agent and element would be employed to lay the oppressor low. Danger and death would hang over their heads day and night. Yes, the tyrants would meet with plagues more terrible than those of Pharaoh. But you are a patient people. You act as though you were made for the special use of these devils. You act as though your daughters were born to pamper the lusts of your masters and overseers. And worse than all, you tamely submit while your lords tear your wives from your embraces and defile them before your eyes. In the name of God, we ask, are you men? Where is the blood of your fathers? Has it all run out of your veins? Awake, awake; millions of voices are calling you! Your dead fathers speak to you from their graves. Heaven, as with a voice of thunder, calls on you to arise from the dust.

Let your motto be resistance! *resistance!* RESISTANCE! No oppressed people have ever secured their liberty without resistance. What kind of resistance you had better make, you must decide by the circumstances that surround you, and according to the suggestion of expediency. Brethren, adieu! Trust in the living God. Labor for the peace of the human race, and remember that you are FOUR MILLIONS.

"This document elicited more discussion than any other paper ever brought before that or any other deliberative body of colored persons and their friends." After listening to all the objections, Mr. Garnet rose and defended the address in what, according to a competent judge, was one of the ablest speeches that ever fell from human lips.* That speech unfortunately is lost, but we have the address; and, after looking over it carefully find it so clear in statement, so compact and thorough in argument, and so radical withal, that it is impossible to select a specimen brick; we give it entire therefore in this volume. Although twenty-two years old, it is good reading to-day. Besides, our brethren, then slaves, and their descendants, are now learning to read all over the land; they will want to preserve this heir-loom of their past condition, and to adopt it as their watchword of conduct should any, under whatever plea or pretext, whether as old masters or new, whether as church or state, whether as friends or *protectors*, attempt to fasten another gyve upon their now fetterless limbs. It is enough to add, that JOHN BROWN having read it, had it with "Walker's Appeal" republished at his own expense.

In January, 1844, Mr. Garnet addressed the Legislature of the State of New York in behalf of equal suffrage.

On 7th July, 1846, he presided at the great gathering of the Delavan Temperance Union, held at Poughkeepsie, and which was attended by steam-boat loads of our people from either direction of the river. In his valedictory, he says:

"Men and women, descendants of Africa: our ancestors were distinguished for their wisdom in the arts and sciences. If you would imitate their good example—if you would find the lost pearl which they treasured up for their children, you must be strangers to the intoxicating cup; for intemperance stupefies the mind and mars its beauty. In the palmy days of our forefathers they were famous for their military achievements, and they wrote their names upon a thousand conquered cities. Let us inscribe ours upon human hearts as friends of temperance and sobriety. All mankind are our brethren. Every good act will add to the treasury of universal benevolence and love. No man however humble or poor is denied the privilege of adding to the common stock. What cannot be done in any other way may be done by example, which is the most salutary of all teachings. * * * I will not recount our

* Dr. Julius Lemoine of Pittsburg, Pa. Major M. R. Delany is the authority for this statement.

wrongs and afflictions in an assembly like this. . It is unnecessary. We all know them and have felt them. If we are sober, industrious, and frugal, we shall be surrounded by a majesty superseding that of monarchs."

"Good Words;" and, it may be, in the possible trials that await our people under reconstruction, a safe-guard for their conduct.

In the autumn of 1846, Gerrit Smith appointed Mr. Garnet one of the agents for distributing his munificent gift of lands among the colored men of his State. It speaks well for his influence and teachings, well for his judgment in selecting beneficiaries, that the largest number of actual occupants of these lands, the best men in overcoming the difficulties in this new and laborious field, and the only men who yet remain there successful cultivators of the soil went from Troy.

The year 1848 terminated Mr. Garnet's residence at Troy, after ten years of arduous labors in the ministry there, resulting in large additions to the number, and advance in the spiritual and social condition of his flock, blessed moreover by mutual love and harmony, and leaving an impress for good which yet survives, he parted with this his first pastoral charge and removed to Geneva. In this city, as in Troy, his labors were abundantly blessed in gathering a large congregation.

The fame of Mr. Garnet's eloquence, his untiring energy and unselfish devotion to the cause of freedom had now reached across the Atlantic, where it created a desire to see and hear him. In 1850 the friends of the Free Labor Movement in Great Britain, and more especially Mrs. Henry Richardson of New Castle-upon-Tyne, invited him over to lecture in behalf of that important portion of the Anti-Slavery cause. Accepting the call, Mr. Garnet went to England, and was in the ensuing year joined by his wife and family. During the ensuing two years and a half he was successfully and almost constantly engaged in the object of his mission. In 1851 he addressed the vast annual gathering at Exeter Hall: and was a delegate to the Peace Congress held at Frankfurt-on-the-Maine, where he was one of the most acceptable speakers. Thence, in company with the late Joseph Sturge of Birmingham, and the widely known Dr. Dick of Broughty Ferry, Scotland, he traveled through Bavaria, Prussia, and France. Returning to England, he divided his time and his labors between the three kingdoms; he had the distinguished honor to preach from the pulpits of the ablest men of the time ; among these may be named Rev. James Sherman, Surrey Chapel, London, and the Rev. Doctors Wardlaw, Eadie and King of Glasgow: he also spoke in the Rotunda, Dublin, and had the good fortune to enjoy the support and friendship of many of the best and most philanthropic personages of the time.

This sojourn in Great Britain was of great service to the good cause and to Mr. Garnet himself. For the cause, it was a continuous and irrefragable argument. The hitherto exhibitions of colored talent had been discounted by the foes, and even by some of the friends, of freedom, on the ground that whatever talent they may have exhibited was due to the white blood in their make-up. They denied the capacity of the pure negro for the higher branches of learning and science. The mouths of all such were closed by the advent of Mr. Garnet. Here was a gentleman of splendid physique, polished manners, extensive learning, well up, especially in English poetry, ably filling the pulpits of their best divines, and bearing off the laurels in eloquence, wit, sarcasm, interlarded with soul-subduing pathos—in short, a master of all the graces of rhetoric—and this gentleman an African of pure lineage, with no admixture of Saxon blood as the source of his unquestionable talent and genius. To be sure, there was the well developed, nearly perpendicular forehead, the long mobile eye-brows, overhanging eyes, that prominent themselves, and like my Lord Stanley's, of irritable leaden hue when in repose, seem almost hidden in the ambush of luxuriant lids, a large nose, like Brougham's, under muscular control, yet hooked as Secretary Seward's, with the short upper lip which Bulwer says is an essential to beauty, a wide but well cut mouth with the thin compressed lips which indicate high determination, and a fighting chin—"all white features," some one will say; not at all; they are the features which God has stamped upon the leaders of mankind in all ages and nations. To Mr. Garnet, it afforded a practical proof of the vincibility of that caste hate against which he had made a life-long struggle, and a strengthening of his soul for a renewal of the fight: and afforded him, while yet on earth, a foretaste of that beatitude, that holy rest for the soul wherein slavery and caste shall be no more. For, if "an undevout astronomer is mad," then, per contra, an intelligent and devout colored clergyman in these United States, believes, in the teeth of a heavier weight of evidence than that which would deny a first cause to be that which places the planets in their orbits, and " bids them roll."

In the latter part of 1852, Mr. Garnet connected himself with the United Presbyterian Church of Scotland, and was sent as a missionary to Sterling. Grange Hill. Jamaica, W. I. In this fine field he was doing successful labor, when his ministry was cut short by a protracted and severe attack of fever; as soon as he became convalescent, he was ordered north by his physicians; returning to New York City, he received a unanimous call in 1855 to Shiloh Church, Prince Street. Hereby he became the successor to his departed friend, the Rev. Theodore S. Wright. The Church had need of him. Circumstances, which need not here be narrated, had reduced it to a mere fragment of its former self, in numbers and good works. Under his energetic ministry it soon revived, and attained, if it did not go beyond, the measure of its best days. The increase in numbers was rapid; at one communion seventy-six persons were added to its fold. The Sunday-school flourished again as of yore, and the various associations,—social, moral, and religious,—which do so much to harmonize and knit the people together lent their aid in advancing the best interests of the church. Their revered pastor, like his distinguished predecessor, kept a vigilant eye upon his young men and women, and encouraged among them efforts for their literary improvement: setting apart, for special culture, those whose gifts seemed best suited to advance the glory of God and the elevation of our people. He did his Master's work wisely and well, and soon became a centre of attraction throughout the city. Every Sunday evening found the capacious aisles of Shiloh filled to overflowing, especially with the most intelligent colored youth of both sexes. His public spirit rapidly attracted to him those of our people, of whatever denomination, who felt desirous to labor for the common good. His well-known patriotism caused his pulpit to be regarded as a pharos in the dim and perilous time that submerged the land in the years preceding and in the early days of the rebellion. The Reporters soon found him out, and put on record his views as an important influence upon the times. Fast days, Proclamation days, the Dred Scott Decision, the martyrdom of John Brown, the fall of Sumter, the Proclamation of Freedom, were some among the many occasions in which his sermons were reported at length in the daily press. They were, all of them, like that printed in this volume, equal to the occasion. He gave forth no uncertain sounds. Penetrated to the very marrow himself, he did not hesitate fearlessly to expose the national sin, and to declare the whole counsel of God to an unrepentant people.

In these manifold labors, the last man thought of by the laborer, was Henry Highland Garnet. He took the lead, to be sure; with that well-marked central feature of his face, how could he do otherwise? What we mean, is, that in these, as in all the labors of his life, he was utterly unselfish. Foxes have holes, birds of the air have nests, but this servant and soldier of Christ—in strict obedience to his Divine Master—has taken no thought of that morrow which age or affliction may bring to his door. He has devoted his life to the service of the people, and his hands are clean.

Any one less pure and unselfish could not have accomplished his mission from 1855 until 1863–64, those long dark hours, whose sorrowful and unmixed gloom preceded the dawn of to-day. The National and State Legislature seemed existent for no other purpose than to enact oppressive laws against us. Commerce turned its otherwise stony front, as if it wished to annihilate us with a frown. The pulpit thundered its anathemas, and mitred prelates held up both hands while they pronounced us cursed in Holy Writ to the doom of chattel-slavery throughout all time. The press, with but few exceptions, hounded on the increasing hatred of the multitude until it found logical expression in the unspeakable atrocities of the New York riots of 1863. Our professed friends, pale with affright, either gave up our cause as hopeless, or shudderingly shut their eyes, if so be to avoid the coming shedding of blood. If any dared lift up voice in our behalf, they were smitten down and beaten like dogs, the most sacred rights, the innermost recesses of the national temple affording them neither safeguard nor refuge. Like a new-born Cain, the hand of every man seemed lifted against us.

Throughout this frightful time, there was at least one black man who neither cowered nor flinched. The tall form of the pastor of Shiloh, always in the front, where blows fell thickest, seemed rather to dilate with the joys of battle, and his voice became as a trumpet's call; by his eloquence, his high-hearted manhood, his conduct and example, he cheered his people, not only his immediate flock, but all who heard him throughout the land. Foot to foot with the common foe, so far from yielding an inch, he steadily advanced, taking newer and, as he believed, broader grounds for our people in whose behalf he claimed perfect equality in all things, until, by what seemed to him a logical necessity, he proclaimed the doctrine of "negro nationality." From this idea grew the organization of the "African Civilization Society," intended to develope the energies of our race wherever found: in the United States, Africa, or elsewhere.

In 1861, as President of this Society, Mr. Garnet re-visited England, and returned the same year.

In the same year, his friends in New York and vicinity, did themselves the honor to make him a handsome present accompanied with appropriate speeches by the eloquent Rev. John T. Raymond, T. G. Campbell, and others. This present consisted of

A silver Tea-set complete.

A silver Salver.

Two Silver Cups.

A Ram's Horn mounted with silver, a token of victory.

A gold mounted Cane.

A Dinner and Tea-set of fine porcelain, consisting of 124 pieces, to Mrs. Garnet.

A parchment containing the names of the donors, upwards of seven hundred in number.

On the breaking out of the rebellion, he called upon our young men to take up arms; and as soon as the government decided to receive colored troops, he volunteered as Chaplain to the colored troops on Riker's Island, under the auspices of the Union Loyal League Club. He served in this capacity until the Twentieth, Twenty-sixth, and Thirty-first Regiments of United States Colored Troops marched to the field. During this time, without interruption of his pastoral duties, he organized a Ladies' Committee for the Aid of Sick Soldiers, and established a hospital kitchen on Riker's Island.

At first, there were difficulties in the way, which interfered with the recruiting of these regiments. The runners kidnapped boys and old men, cripples and maimed, and by collusion with the proper officers, forced them to Riker's Island. Here the sutlers charged fifty cents for a cup of coffee, a dollar for a canteen of water; in the cold month of February they were thrust into old and worn cotton tents, compelled to sleep on the earth without even a camp-stool. How these difficulties

8

were met and overcome is told in the "Report of the Committee on Recruiting of the Union League Club," p. 38. "These three things—the public meetings in colored churches, attended in person by members of the Committee; the printing of circulars, with the names of distinguished colored men,[*] side by side with those of the Committee; and the employing of the able and faithful friend of their race, Rev. Mr. Garnet, to visit Riker's Island and hear the complaints of the recruits and getting General Dix to right them, soon secured the confidence of the colored people in our patriotic enterprise.

"Recruits in large numbers came quickly in. Among the volunteers enlisting were men from the British West India Islands, Hayti, Canada, Maryland, Virginia, Kentucky, and the West; but the majority were found the respectable, industrious and hard-working classes of our own State and city. And as colored soldiers were a new feature in the war, their march to and from headquarters through the streets of the city, created quite a sensation. Occasional signs of disrespect were noticed, but much oftener they were greeted with hearty approbation."

"Hearty approbation!" In the streets of New York, in February, 1864; what a wide contrast to what occurred in these same streets only seven months before, in July, 1863. Well might it have been said to the colored people

> " God moves in a mysterious way
> His wonders to perform."

To have been mobbed, hunted down, beaten to death, hung to the lamp-posts or trees, burned, their dwellings sacked and destroyed, their orphan children turned homeless from their comfortable shelter which was destroyed by fire, and then, within a few months to be cheered along the same streets, are occurrences whose happening put ordinary miracles in the shade; the first, more hideous than hell; the last, one which might be, and was smiled on by heaven.

The Rev. Mr. Garnet was too prominently known to escape the attention of the July rioters: they rushed down Thirtieth Street where he resided, loudly calling him by name. By the lucky forethought of his daughter who wrenched off the door-plate with an axe, his house escaped

---

[*] Rev. Henry Highland Garnet, Rev. Clinton Leonard, Rev. John Cary, Rev. Henry M. Wilson, Rev. R. H. Cain, Rev. S. Talbot, Rev. James N. Gloucester, Mr. S. N. Gibbs.

sacking, and his own life and that of his family were preserved by the kind acts of some white neighbors.

Within five days of the commencement of the riot, and before it was thoroughly subdued, the merchants of New York organized a committee for the relief of the colored sufferers. They established an office at 350 Fourth Street, to which all applicants for aid were directed to apply. They wisely engaged the services of the Rev. H. H. Garnet at this office, in order that he might examine and report on each case that came up. During the month ending, August 21st, 1863, not less than 6,392 persons passed under his supervision, and were relieved. At the conclusion of these labors, Mr. Garnet wrote the following address to the committee:

## ACKNOWLEDGMENT FROM THE COLORED PEOPLE.

On Saturday, August 22d, a number of the leading colored clergymen and laymen assembled together, and, unexpectedly to the committee, presented them with the following address, elaborately engrossed on parchment, and tastefully framed—the engrossing being the work of Mr. Patrick Reason, one of their own people.

## AN ADDRESS

### TO THE EXECUTIVE COMMITTEE OF MERCHANTS FOR THE RELIEF OF COLORED PEOPLE.

J. D. McKENZIE, Chairman.

| | |
|---|---|
| Edward Cromwell, | George C. Collins, |
| J. S. Schultz, | A. R. Wetmore, |
| Jona. Sturges, Treas., | J. B. Collins. |

PRESENTED BY

## COLORED MINISTERS AND LAYMEN.

New York, Aug. 22, 1863.

Gentlemen:—We have learned that you have decided this day to bring to a close the general distribution of the funds so liberally contributed by the merchants of New York and others for the relief of the colored sufferers of the late riots, which have recently disgraced our city.

We cannot, in justice to our feelings, permit your benevolent labors to terminate, even partially, without offering some expression of our sincere gratitude to the universal Father for inspiring your hearts with that spirit of kindness of which we have been the recipients during the severe trials and persecutions through which we have passed.

When in the pursuit of our peaceful and humble occupations we had fallen among thieves, who stripped us of our raiment and had wounded us, leaving many of us half dead, you had compassion on us. You bound up our wounds and poured in the oil and wine of Christian kindness and took care of us. You hastened to express your sympathy for those whose fathers, husbands, sons and brothers had been tortured and murdered. You also comforted the aching hearts of our widowed sisters and soothed the sorrows of orphan children.

We were hungry and you fed us. We were thirsty and you gave us drink. We were made as strangers in our own homes and you kindly took us in. We were naked and you clothed us. We were sick and you visited us. We were in prison and you came unto us.

Gentlemen, this generation of our people will not, cannot forget the scenes to which we allude, nor will they forget the noble and spontaneous exhibition of charity which they excited. The former will be referred to as one of the dark chapters of our history in the Empire State, and the latter will be remembered as a bright and glorious page in the records of the past.

In the light of public opinion we feel ourselves to be among the least in this our native land, and we therefore earnestly pray that in the last great day the King may say to you and to all who have befriended us, "Inasmuch as you have done it to one of the least of these my brethren you have done it unto me; come ye blessed of my Father inherit the kingdom prepared for you from the foundation of the world."

But as great as has been the benefit that we have received from your friendly and unlooked for charity, they yet form but the smaller portion of the ground of our gratitude and pleasure. We have learned by your treatment of us in these days of our mental and physical affliction, that you cherished for us a kindly and humane feeling of which we had no knowledge. You did not hesitate to come forward to our relief amid threatened destruction of your own lives and property. You obeyed the noblest dictates of the human heart, and by your generous moral courage you rolled back the tide of violence that had well nigh swept us away.

This ever memorable and magnanimous exhibition of heroism has had the effect to enlarge in our bosoms the sentiment of undying regard and esteem for you and yours. In time of war or peace, in prosperity or in adversity, you and our great State and our beloved country may count us among your faithful friends, and the proffer of our labors and our lives shall be our pleasure and our pride.

If, in your temporary labors of Christian philanthropy, you have been induced to look forward to our future destiny in this our native land, and to ask what is the best thing that we can do for the colored people, this is our answer:—Protect us in our endeavors to obtain an honest living—suffer no one to hinder us in any department of well directed industry, give us a fair and open field and let us work out our own destiny, and we ask no more.

We cannot conclude without expressing our gratification at the manner in which the arduous and perplexing duties of your office have been conducted; we shall never forget the Christian and gentlemanly bearing of your esteemed Secretary, Mr. VINCENT COLYER, who on all occasions impressed even the humblest with the belief that he knew and felt that he was dealing with a crushed and heart-broken people.

We also acknowledge the uniform kindness and courtesy that has characterized the conduct of all the gentlemen in the office in the discharge of their duties.

We desire likewise to acknowledge the valuable services contributed by the gentlemen of the legal profession, who have daily been in attendance at the office to make out the claims of the sufferers *free of charge*. In the name of the people we return thanks to all.

In conclusion permit us to assure you that we will never cease to pray to God for your prosperity, and that of every donor to the Relief Fund. Also for the permanent peace of our country, based upon liberty, and the enjoyment of man's inalienable rights, for the preservation of the

American Union, and for the reign of that righteousness in the hearts of the people, that saves from reproach and exalteth the nation.

Signed,

| | | | |
|---|---|---|---|
| Rev. H. H. Garnet, | | Mr. John Peterson, |
| " | Chas. B. Ray, | " | Chas. L. Reason, |
| " | Clinton Leonard, | " | Peter S. Porter, |
| " | John Cary, | " | Stephen N. Gear, |
| " | Henry M. Wilson, | " | Hy. Montgomery, |
| " | Sampson Talbot, | " | John L. Hudson, |
| " | Richard Wilson, | " | Aaron F. Potter, |
| " | Isaac Colman, | " | T. S. W. Titus, |
| " | John T. Raymond, | " | Wm. C. H. Curtis, |

And many others.

To this Address the chairman of the committee responded.

By a vote of the Executive Committee, Mr. McKenzie was requested to furnish a copy of his remarks for publication, which are herewith appended.

## REPLY OF THE CHAIRMAN,
### Mr. J. D. McKenzie.

"Although entirely unprepared, it becomes my duty as chairman of the Executive Committee appointed by the merchants of New York for the relief of the colored people, who suffered by the recent mob, to respond to the address, which you have this morning presented to us in behalf of your people.

"It is unnecessary for me to go over the origin of the movement, or the manner in which it has been conducted; these things you know. But I would say that to many of our number it has been a new and profitable experience, one which we can never forget as our memory goes back to those dark hours when your kindred fled in terror and dismay from before those who murdered and pillaged your homes, men who had in the majority of cases come from other lands, who had received protection under our laws both in their persons and property, who from dependence and poverty had become independent in their circumstances, with an abundance for themselves and their families, with every right both civil and political enjoyed by the most favored citizen, and who sought to destroy a race cast upon our care and protection by the

great God who made of one blood all the nations of men to dwell upon
the face of the earth. Our whole natures revolted instantly at so great
and cruel wrong. For this we claim no credit, it was only the common
instinct of humanity when we heard the imploring wail of an injured
and dependent race ringing in our ears imploringly for mercy—aye, and
they shall have it, and justice also; to this the merchants of New York
are fully and completely pledged by their words and their acts—this is
what every man who treads this soil should in time to come receive not
as a favor, but a right.

"Some of us have been told that if we stood forth in your behalf our
stores and our houses would be burned, and our lives taken: if this
must be the penalty, let it come; with God's help we will build other
stores and make new homes: and if life must be yielded and we die for
a principle of justice and truth, then shall our death be more glorious
than our life.

"We hope that the colored people in time to come, from the experience of the past few weeks, will trust the white man as their friend.
Their condition and their future is a problem to us of momentous importance—it engages our thoughts, I am well convinced, far more than it
possibly can your own; it is the great question of the age. Go where
we may the black man does not escape us—when we sit at our tables
surrounded by our families—although you are not personally present in
bodily shape still you are there—when we retire to our chambers you
follow us—and even in the sanctuary of the Most High the question will
come without bidding to every heart, what shall be done with the negro? Human wisdom is utterly unable to solve the proposition; God in
his providence alone can do it. For myself I had hoped that your race
would have been gradually emancipated, first being prepared for the enjoyment of liberty and the discharge of the duties and obligations at-
tendant thereon; but God, who controls all events according as he sees
fit, in his own infinite wisdom, seems to our present view to order
otherwise, and it is our duty to accept his will as right.

"Twice in the world's history has he signally interposed in behalf of
the enslaved. Once in generations long gone by with the years after
the flood when his people Israel were under the yoke of the Egyptians—
he brought them forth with a mighty hand and an outstretched arm.
He told that haughty nation these words, 'Let my people go free.'
This they refused, until finally there was no home among the Egyptians

in which on that eventful night there were not cries and lamentations over the dead body of the first-born son.

"Three years ago we little thought that we should for a like cause learn over again the same lesson. There is hardly a family circle at the North, and almost certainly there is not one at the South, where the mother does not mourn over the dead boy, or where the wife has not been made a widow, and all this has come to us because your people dwelt among us—the innocent cause of untold woes. We know full well that you and yours are not responsible for these calamities. It seems to me that, disguise it as we may, slavery in these United States is doomed. It may not end this year nor the next, but end it will, and that speedily; a voice rings through the air clearer and louder than the loudest thunders: 'Let the oppressed go free.'

"And now in view of all these things, of your approaching state, suffer me through you to speak a few words of counsel and advice to your race. The path before you is full of difficulty and dangers; when you come into the full possession of liberty, remember that true liberty is not licentiousness—it is obedience to law—it is a cheerful compliance with the obligations imposed by society for the good of the whole—it is rendering to every man his due.

"You will go forth without any claims upon society beyond those conceded to every man—you will meet at the outset a haughty, powerful and energetic race—a race which to-day rules and controls all others. Can you stand before the Anglo-Saxon and Celtic tribes? The ordeal before you is a fearful one.

"Your only hope can be in fearing and obeying God's law, in industry, virtue and education; these things only can save your people; otherwise you will melt away when cast upon your own resources, faster than the snow in summer, or the dew which glistens for a little while on the flowers of the morning: it cannot in the nature of the case be otherwise.

"But I must conclude. The labor in which we have been engaged as a committee of the merchants of New York, has been to us not only pleasant, but also profitable; we had nothing to gain but your good. We were impelled to this work by the remembrance of how much we have ourselves received, how much God has blessed and prospered us in this goodly land, unworthy though we were of these blessings; but more than all we were constrained to do these things because of God's greatest gift to man, Jesus Christ his only Son, who gave himself to redeem a lost and guilty world—as children of one Common Father who makes his sun to shine alike on every tribe of man. The words of John the beloved apostle come to my mind when he describes the day of all days in those magnificent words, 'After this, I beheld, and lo, a great multitude, which no man could number, of all nations, and kindreds, and people, and tongues, stood before the throne and before the Lamb, clothed with white robes, and palms in their hands, and they sang a new song.' Then shall the nations see eye to eye—there shall all distinctions end—there shall be but one language and one harmony when earth's ransomed ones shall be all safely gathered in that better land."

In April, 1864, the Rev. Mr. Garnet received a unanimous call to the Fifteenth Street Presbyterian Church, Washington, D. C., and he entered upon his duties there (where he is still engaged) in June following. It may not be generally known that up to that date, and for nearly a year afterwards, no man of color was allowed to set his foot inside the National Halls of Legislature: the high places where his chains were forged were hidden behind the veil, and from his sight, by express enactment: the evil doers rightly hid from their victims the scene of their evil deeds. The hell of hells, where God's poor, by fitting rites were seared out of their manhood, where Christianity, Human Brotherhood, Common Humanity and every link which binds society together were ruthlessly gainsayed, scorned and broken, could not brook the noon-day gaze of the injured black man.

It is one among the most prominent proofs of the change that has come over public sentiment, that in one of these very halls, without any seeking on his part, on the contrary at the request of several Representatives, our reverend friend is requested by the Chaplain in charge to preach.

On the 12th of February, 1865, at the request of the Chaplain, the Rev. Wm. H. Channing. the Rev. Henry H. Garnet preached to an overflowing audience in the House of Representatives, Washington. D. C. The following, from the pen of an eye-witness,* gives an admirable description of the scene:

"I arrived at the Hall of Representatives, at 11 A. M., and found

* Mr. William J. Wilson, formerly of Brooklyn, now of Washington, D. C.

9

every seat upon the floor occupied, and the galleries filled to overflowing. "The choir of the Rev. gentleman's church, which, by the way, is one of the very best we have in the country, was also invited to serve on this occasion, and crowned itself with honor. It was a strange sight, in the presence of the assembled wisdom, and, I may add, if not of the old prejudice, certainly of the feeling which always succeeds it—it was a strange sight, I say, to see this little band of vocalists, stand up in places where but one year ago only white persons were allowed to stand, and there chant up hymns of praise to God for his goodness and his wonderful works to the children of men; and it was a sight stranger still to see this colored divine stand up in the dignity of his high office as a priest of the Most High in that Speaker's desk.

"But, we are assembled ; white and colored—all mingled and all seemingly comfortable. Perhaps it is always thus when we occupy the highest places at the *feast*. It is then, that our white friends, even the most fastidious of them, feel truly comfortable, and it is only natural that they should. But we are all seated, or positioned on our feet, as the case may be, and are as still as the lake at even-tide. All eyes are turned toward the reverend gentleman, who in that quiet dignity which impresses every one, rose and offered up a fervent prayer to the throne of Grace. His words were unction, and I have wondered, who of that vast assembly were not touched by their pathetic wail as they came forth from one who wrestled with an angel. The preacher then read the first hymn,

'All hail the power of Jesus' name.'

Then followed the reading of the Scriptures. Then all eyes were turned towards the choir as in sweet and touching melody it warbled forth the beautiful sentiment,

'Arise, my soul, shake off thy fears.'

And now the text is read ; from the choir back again to the clergyman, attention is turned as a wheat-field upon a sudden change of wind. All the attention which that vast congregation can give, is, unreservedly at the speaker's command, while he proceeds to unfold the text, make plain its meaning, and apply its divine teachings to the hearts and understandings of his hearers. For the space of an hour what a breathless house! What suppressed emotions!

"Breathless house, did I say? When standing in the Speaker's place, with the full length portrait of Washington on his right and that of Lafayette on his left, the eloquent preacher appealed as authority to both 'that our land was made for free men and free women,' the silence was broken, and, but for the Sabbath morning the restrained applause would have been unbounded: so also when, in a sudden outburst, he exclaimed, 'Should any poet have attempted to write in praise of American Slavery, the ink would have frozen upon the point of his pen!' and, too, in his tribute to Washington, Jefferson, and Adams, and the host of freedom's champions who have passed away, a thrill ran through the house which surpassed all the applause I have ever heard. When he said, 'These worthies, if they looked down on the scene which transpired in this hall a few days since, when the great National Work was consummated, they must have responded, with the angel choir, a hearty amen!' an uncontrollable emotion, for the moment, took entire possession of the audience.

"It is needless to say more. Men who went to the house to hear a colored man, came away having heard a MAN in the highest and fullest sense. Many who went there with feelings of curiosity, came away wrapped in astonishment. Not only a man, but a great representative man had spoken, and they were amazed."

We have now laid before the reader, a brief and imperfect sketch of the life of the Rev. Henry Highland Garnet, believing it to be the best introduction to the sermon, able and eloquent in itself, and historic in the occasion and place of its delivery. For more than the third of the present century Mr. Garnet has been a worker, for a full fourth of the century a prominent leader among his down-trodden brethren. If in giving an account of his life, there seems, to some, to be manifold digressions into the passing events, it is because he was so much mixed up with and a part of these events that to separate him from them would be manifestly impossible. The simple narrative of his labors is the highest praise that can be bestowed upon him; so earnest, so zealous, so true, so constantly on the watch-tower, ready to sound the first alarm, ready to receive or ward off or strike the first blow, we have come to look up to him as our natural, our appointed leader.

At least this may be said of him, of his brilliant talents he has made the best, the fullest use, for the benefit of a peeled, down-trodden and despised race; what his hand has found to do, he has done with his might. At the present moment, so full of important issues to the people who are his people, his residence by Divine permission, is at the National Capital, where his opportunities to watch and labor are greatly increased, and the responsibilities resting upon him more than doubled; there is no doubt that he will do his duty; but should not the people also strengthen his hands, as the whites strengthen the hands of their leaders?

# DISCOURSE.

MATTHEW xxiii. 4: "For they bind heavy burdens, and grievous to be borne, and lay them on men's shoulders, but they themselves will not move them with one of their fingers."

In this chapter, of which my text is a sentence, the Lord Jesus addressed his disciples, and the multitude that hung spell-bound upon the words that fell from his lips. He admonished them to beware of the religion of the Scribes and Pharisees, which was distinguished for great professions, while it succeeded in urging them to do but a little, or nothing that accorded with the law of righteousness.

In theory they were right; but their practices were inconsistent and wrong. They were learned in the law of Moses, and in the traditions of their fathers, but the principles of righteousness failed to affect their hearts. They knew their duty, but did it not. The demands which they made upon others proved that they themselves knew what things men ought to do. In condemning others they pronounced themselves guilty. They demanded that others should be just. merciful, pure, peaceable, and righteous. But they were unjust, impure, unmerciful—they hated and wronged a portion of their fellow-men, and waged continual war against the government of God.

On other men's shoulders they bound heavy and grievous burdens of duties and obligations. The people groaned beneath the loads which were imposed upon them, and in bitterness of spirit cried out, and filled the land with lamentations. But, with their eyes closed, and their hearts hardened, they heeded not, neither did they care. They regarded it to be but little less than intolerable insult to be asked to bear a small portion of the burdens which they were swift to bind on the shoulders of their fellow-men. With loud voice, and proud and defiant mien, they said these burdens are for them, and not for us. Behold how patiently they bear them. Their shoulders are broad, and adapted to the condition to which we have doomed them. But as for us, it is irksome, even to adjust their burdens, though we see them stagger beneath them.

Such was their conduct in the Church and in the State. We have modern Scribes and Pharisees, who are faithful to their prototypes of ancient times.

With sincere respect and reverence for the instruction, and the warning given by our Lord, and in humble dependence upon him for his assistance, I shall speak this morning of the Scribes and Pharisees of our times who rule the State. In discharging this duty, I shall keep my eyes upon the picture which is painted so faithfully and life-like by the hand of the Saviour.

Allow me to describe them. They are intelligent and well-informed, and can never say, either before an earthly tribunal or at the bar of God, "*We knew not of ourselves what was right.*" They are acquainted with the principles of the law of nations. They are proficient in the knowledge of Constitutional law. They are teachers of common law, and frame and execute statute law. They acknowledge that there is a just and impartial God, and are not altogether unacquainted with the law of Christian love and kindness. They claim for themselves the broadest freedom. Boastfully they tell us that they have received from the court of heaven the MAGNA CHARTA of human rights that was handed down through the clouds, and amid the lightnings of Sinai. and given again by the Son of God on the Mount of Beatitudes, while the glory of the Father shone around him. They tell us that from the Declaration of Independence and the Constitution they have obtained a guaranty of their political freedom, and from the Bible they derive their claim to all the blessings of religious liberty. With just pride they tell us that they are descended from the Pilgrims, who threw themselves upon the bosom of the treacherous sea. and braved storms and tempests, that they might find in a strange land, and among savages, free homes, where they might build their altars that should blaze with acceptable sacrifice unto God. Yes! they boast that their fathers heroically turned away from the precious light of Eastern civilization, and taking their lamps with oil in their vessels, joyfully went forth to illuminate this land, that then dwelt in the darkness of the valley of the shadow of death. With hearts strengthened by faith they spread out their standard to the winds of heaven, near Plymouth rock; and whether it was stiffened in the sleet and frosts of winter, or floated on the breeze of summer, it ever bore the motto, " *Freedom to worship God.*"

But others, their fellow-men, equal before the Almighty, and made by him of the same blood, and glowing with immortality, they doom to life-long servitude and chains. Yes, they stand in the most sacred places on earth, and beneath the gaze of the piercing eye of Jehovah, the universal Father of all men, and declare, " *that the best possible condition of the negro is slavery.*"*

> "Thus man devotes his brother and destroys;
> And more than all, and most to be deplored,
> As human nature's broadest, foulest blot,
> Chains him, and tasks him, and exacts his sweat
> With stripes, that Mercy with bleeding heart,
> Weeps to see inflicted on a beast."

In the name of the TRIUNE GOD I denounce the

* Speech of FERNANDO WOOD, of New York, in Congress, 1864.

sentiment as unrighteous beyond measure, and the holy and the just of the whole earth say in regard to it, Anathema-maranatha.

What is slavery? Too well do I know what it is. I will present to you a bird's-eye view of it; and it shall be no fancy picture, but one that is sketched by painful experience. I was born among the cherished institutions of slavery. My earliest recollections of parents, friends, and the home of my childhood are clouded with its wrongs. The first sight that met my eyes was a Christian mother enslaved by professed Christians, but, thank God, now a saint in heaven. The first sounds that startled my ear, and sent a shudder through my soul, were the cracking of the whip, and the clanking of chains. These sad memories mar the beauties of my native shores, and darken all the slave-land, which, but for the reign of despotism, had been a paradise. But those shores are fairer now. The mists have left my native valleys, and the clouds have rolled away from the hills, and Maryland, the unhonored grave of my fathers, is now the free home of their liberated and happier children.

Let us view this demon, which the people have worshiped as a God. Come forth, thou grim monster, that thou mayest be critically examined! There he stands. Behold him, one and all. Its work is to chattleize man; to hold property in human beings. Great God! I would as soon attempt to enslave GA-

10

BRIEL or MICHAEL as to enslave a man made in the image of God, and for whom Christ died. Slavery is snatching man from the high place to which he was lifted by the hand of God, and dragging him down to the level of the brute creation, where he is made to be the companion of the horse and the fellow of the ox.

It tears the crown of glory from his head, and as far as possible obliterates the image of God that is in him. Slavery preys upon man, and man only. A brute cannot be made a slave. Why? Because a brute has not reason, faith, nor an undying spirit, nor conscience. It does not look forward to the future with joy or fear, nor reflect upon the past with satisfaction or regret. But who in this vast assembly, who in all this broad land, will say that the poorest and most unhappy brother in chains and servitude has not every one of these high endowments? Who denies it? Is there one? If so, let him speak. There is not one; no, not one.

But slavery attempts to make a man a brute. It treats him as a beast. Its terrible work is not finished until the ruined victim of its lusts, and pride, and avarice, and hatred, is reduced so low that with tearful eyes and feeble voice he faintly cries, "*I am happy and contented—I love this condition.*"

"Proud Nimrod first the bloody chase began.
A mighty hunter he; his prey was man."

The caged lion may cease to roar, and try no longer

the strength of the bars of his prison, and lie with his head between his mighty paws and snuff the polluted air as though he heeded not. But is he contented? Does he not instinctively long for the freedom of the forest and the plain? Yes, he is a lion still. Our poor and forlorn brother whom thou hast labelled "*slave*," is also a man. He may be unfortunate, weak, helpless, and despised, and hated, nevertheless he is a man. His God and thine has stamped on his forehead his title to his inalienable rights in characters that can be read by every intelligent being. Pitiless storms of outrage may have beaten upon his defenceless head, and he may have descended through ages of oppression, yet he is a man. God made him such, and his brother cannot unmake him. Woe, woe to him who attempts to commit the accursed crime.

Slavery commenced its dreadful work in kidnapping unoffending men in a foreign and distant land, and in piracy on the seas. The plunderers were not the followers of Mahomet, nor the devotees of Hindooism, nor benighted pagans, nor idolaters, but people called Christians, and thus the ruthless traders in the souls and bodies of men fastened upon Christianity a crime and stain at the sight of which it shudders and shrieks.

It is guilty of the most heinous iniquities ever perpetrated upon helpless women and innocent children. Go to the shores of the land of my forefathers, poor bleeding Africa, which, although she has been bereaved, and robbed for centuries, is nevertheless beloved by all her worthy descendants wherever dispersed. Behold a single scene that there meets your eyes. Turn not away neither from shame, pity, nor indifference, but look and see the beginning of this cherished and petted institution. Behold a hundred youthful mothers seated on the ground, dropping their tears upon the hot sands, and filling the air with their lamentations.

Why do they weep? Ah, Lord God, thou knowest! Their babes have been torn from their bosoms and cast upon the plains to die of hunger, or to be devoured by hyenas or jackals. The little innocents would die on the "Middle Passage," or suffocate between the decks of the floating slave-pen, freighted and packed with unparalleled human woe, and the slavers in mercy have cast them out to perish on their native shores. Such is the beginning, and no less wicked is the end of that system which the Scribes and Pharisees in the Church and the State pronounce to be just, humane, benevolent and Christian. If such are the deeds of mercy wrought by angels, then tell me what works of iniquity there remain for devils to do?

This commerce in human beings has been carried on until three hundred thousand have been dragged from their native land in a single year. While this foreign trade has been pursued, who can calculate the enormities and extent of the domestic traffic which has flourished in every slave State, while the whole country has been open to the hunters of men.

It is the highly concentrated essence of all conceivable wickedness. Theft, robbery, pollution, unbridled passion, incest, cruelty, cold-blooded murder, blasphemy, and defiance of the laws of God. It teaches children to disregard parental authority. It tears down the marriage altar, and tramples its sacred ashes under its feet. It creates and nourishes polygamy. It feeds and pampers its hateful handmaid, prejudice.

It has divided our national councils. It has engendered deadly strife between brethren. It has wasted the treasure of the Commonwealth, and the lives of thousands of brave men, and driven troops of helpless women and children into yawning tombs. It has caused the bloodiest civil war recorded in the book of time. It has shorn this nation of its locks of strength that was rising as a young lion in the Western world. It has offered us as a sacrifice to the jealousy and cupidity of tyrants, despots, and adventurers of foreign countries. It has opened a door through which a usurper, a perjured, but a powerful prince, might stealthily enter and build an empire on the golden borders of our southwestern frontier, and which is but a stepping-stone to further and unlimited conquests on this continent. It has desolated the fairest portions of our land, " until the wolf long since driven back by the march of civilization returns after the lapse of a hundred years and howls amidst its ruins."

It seals up the Bible, and mutilates its sacred truths, and flies into the face of the Almighty, and impiously asks, "*Who art thou that I should obey thee?*" Such are the outlines of this fearful national sin; and yet the condition to which it reduces man, it is affirmed, is the best that can possibly be devised for him.

When inconsistencies similar in character, and no more glaring, passed beneath the eye of the Son of God, no wonder he broke forth in language of vehement denunciation. Ye Scribes, Pharisees, and hypocrites! Ye blind guides! Ye compass sea and land to make one proselyte, and when he is made ye make him twofold more the child of hell than yourselves. Ye are like unto whited sepulchres, which indeed appear beautiful without, but within are full of dead men's bones, and all uncleanness!

Let us here take up the golden rule, and adopt the self-application mode of reasoning to those who hold these erroneous views. Come, gird up thy loins and answer like a man, if thou canst. Is slavery, as it is seen in its origin, continuance, and end the best possible condition for thee? Oh, no! Wilt thou bear that burden on thy shoulders, which thou wouldest lay upon thy fellow-man? No. Wilt thou bear a part of it, or remove a little of its weight with one of thy fingers? The sharp and indignant answer is no, no! Then how, and when, and where, shall we apply to thee the golden rule, which says, "*Therefore all things that ye would that others should do to you, do ye even so unto them, for this is the law and the prophets.*"

Let us have the testimony of the wise and great of ancient and modern times:

"Sages who wrote and warriors who bled."

PLATO declared that "Slavery is a system of complete injustice."

SOCRATES wrote that "Slavery is a system of outrage and robbery."

CYRUS said, "To fight in order not to be a slave is noble."

If Cyrus had lived in our land a few years ago he would have been arrested for using incendiary language, and for inciting servile insurrection, and the royal fanatic would have been hanged on a gallows higher than Haman. But every man is fanatical when his soul is warmed by the generous fires of liberty. Is it then truly noble to fight in order not to be a slave? The Chief Magistrate of the nation, and our rulers, and all truly patriotic men think so; and so think legions of black men, who for a season were scorned and rejected, but who came quickly and cheerfully when they were at last invited, bearing a heavy burden of proscriptions upon their shoulders, and having faith in God, and in their generous fellow-countrymen, they went forth to fight a double battle. The foes of their country were before them, while the enemies of freedom and of their race surrounded them.

Augustine, Constantine, Ignatius, Polycarp, Maximus, and the most illustrious lights of the ancient church denounced the sin of slave-holding.

Thomas Jefferson said at a period of his life, when his judgment was matured, and his experience was ripe, "There is preparing, I hope, under the auspices of heaven, a way for a total emancipation."

The sainted Washington said, near the close of his mortal career, and when the light of eternity was beaming upon him, "It is among my first wishes to see some plan adopted by which slavery in this country shall be abolished by law. I know of but one way by which this can be done, and that is by legislative action, and so far as my vote can go, it shall not be wanting."

The other day, when the light of Liberty streamed through this marble pile, and the hearts of the noble band of patriotic statesmen leaped for joy, and this our national capital shook from foundation to dome with the shouts of a ransomed people, then methinks the spirits of Washington, Jefferson, the Jays, the Adamses, and Franklin, and Lafayette, and Giddings, and Lovejoy, and those of all the mighty, and glorious dead, remembered by history, because they were faithful to truth, justice, and liberty, were hovering over the august assembly. Though unseen by mortal eyes, doubtless they joined the angelic choir, and said, Amen.

POPE LEO X. testifies, "That not only does the Christian religion, but nature herself, cry out against a state of slavery."

PATRICK HENRY said, "We should transmit to posterity our abhorrence of slavery." So also thought the Thirty-Eighth Congress.

LAFAYETTE proclaimed these words: "Slavery is a dark spot on the face of the nation." God be praised, that stain will soon be wiped out.

JONATHAN EDWARDS declared "that to hold a man in slavery is to be every day guilty of robbery, or of man stealing."

Rev. Dr. WILLIAM ELLERY CHANNING, in a *Letter on the Annexation of Texas in* 1837, writes as follows:

"The evil of slavery speaks for itself. To state is to condemn the institution. The choice which every freeman makes of death for his child and for everything he loves in preference to slavery, shows what it is. The single consideration that by slavery one human being is placed powerless and defenceless in the hands of another to be driven to whatever labor that other may impose, to suffer whatever punishment he may inflict, to live as his tool, the instrument of his pleasure, this is all that is needed to satisfy such as know the human heart and its unfitness for irresponsible power, that of all conditions slavery is the most hostile to the dignity, self-respect, improvement, rights, and happiness of human beings. * * * Every principle of our government and religion condemns slavery. The spirit of our age condemns it. The decree of the civilized world has gone out against it. * * * Is there an age in which a free and Christian people shall deliberately resolve to extend and perpetuate the evil? In so doing we cut ourselves off from the communion of nations; we sink below the civilization of our age; we invite the scorn, indignation, and abhorrence of the world."

MOSES, the greatest of all lawgivers and legislators, said, while his face was yet radiant with the light of Sinai: "Whoso stealeth a man, and selleth him, or if he be found in his hand, he shall surely be put to death." The destroying angel has gone forth through this land to execute the fearful penalties of God's broken law.

The Representatives of the nation have bowed with reverence to the Divine edict, and laid the axe at the root of the tree, and thus saved succeeding generations from the guilt of oppression, and from the wrath of God.

Statesmen, Jurists, and Philosophers, most renowned for learning, and most profound in every department of science and literature, have testified against slavery. While oratory has brought its costliest, golden treasures, and laid them on the altar of God and of freedom, it has aimed its fiercest lightning and loudest thunder at the strongholds of tyranny, injustice, and despotism.

From the days of Balak to those of Isaiah and Jeremiah, up to the times of Paul, and through every age of the Christian Church, the sons of thunder have denounced the abominable thing. The heroes who stood in the shining ranks of the hosts of the friends of human progress, from Cicero to Chatham, and Burke, Sharp, Wilberforce, and Thomas Clarkson, and Curran, assaulted the citadel of despotism. The orators and statesmen of our own land, whether they belong to the past, or to the present age, will live and shine in the annals of history, in proportion as they have dedicated their genius and talents to the defence of Justice and man's God-given rights.

All the poets who live in sacred and profane history have charmed the world with their most enchanting strains, when they have tuned their lyres to the praise of Liberty. When the Muses can no longer decorate her altars with their garlands, then they hang their harps upon the willows and weep.

From Moses to Terence and Homer, from thence to Milton and Cowper, Thomson and Thomas Campbell, and on to the days of our own bards, our Bryants, Longfellows, Whittiers, Morrises, and Bokers, all have presented their best gifts to the interests and rights of man.

Every good principle, and every great and noble power, have been made the subjects of the inspired verse, and the songs of poets. But who of them has attempted to immortalize slavery? You will search in vain the annals of the world to find an instance. Should any attempt the sacrilegious work, his genius would fall to the earth as if smitten by the lightning of heaven. Should he lift his hand to write a line in its praise, or defence, the ink would freeze on the point of his pen.

Could we array in one line, representatives of all the families of men, beginning with those lowest in the scale of being, and should we put to them the question. Is it right and desirable that you should be reduced to the condition of slaves, to be registered with chattels, to have your persons, and your lives, and the products of your labor, subjected to the will and the interests of others? Is it right and just that the persons of your wives and children should be at the disposal of others, and be yielded to them for the purpose of pampering their lusts and greed of gain? Is it right to lay heavy burdens on other men's shoulders which you would not remove with one of your fingers? From the rude savage and barbarian the negative response would come, increasing in power and significance as it rolled up the line. And when those should reply, whose minds and hearts are illuminated with the highest civilization and with the spirit of Christianity, the answer deep-toned and prolonged would thunder forth, no, no!

With all the moral attributes of God on our side, cheered as we are by the voices of universal human nature,—in view of the best interests of the present and future generations—animated with the noble desire to furnish the nations of the earth with a worthy example, let the verdict of death which has been brought in against slavery, by the THIRTY-EIGHTH CONGRESS, be affirmed and executed by the people. Let the gigantic monster perish. Yes, perish now, and perish forever!

> "Down let the shrine of Moloch sink,
>     And leave no traces where it stood ;
> No longer let its idol drink,
>     His daily cup of human blood.
> But rear another altar there,
>     To truth, and love, and mercy given,
> And freedom's gift and freedom's prayer,
>     Shall call an answer down from heaven."

It is often asked when and where will the demands of the reformers of this and coming ages end? It is a fair question, and I will answer.

When all unjust and heavy burdens shall be removed from every man in the land. When all invidious and proscriptive distinctions shall be blotted out from our laws, whether they be constitutional, statute, or municipal laws. When emancipation shall be followed by enfranchisement, and all men holding allegiance to the government shall enjoy every right of American citizenship. When our brave and gallant soldiers shall have justice done unto them. When the men who endure the sufferings and perils of the battle-field in the defence of their country, and in order to keep our rulers in their places, shall enjoy the well-earned privilege of voting for them. When in the army and navy, and in every legitimate and honorable occupation, promotion shall smile upon merit without the slightest regard to the complexion of a man's face. When there shall be no more class-legislation, and no more trouble concerning the black man and his rights, than there is in regard to other American citizens. When, in every respect, he shall be equal before the law, and shall be left to make his own way in the social walks of life.

We ask, and only ask, that when our poor frail barks are launched on life's ocean—

"Bound on a voyage of awful length
And dangers little known,"

that, in common with others, we may be furnished with rudder, helm, and sails, and charts, and compass. Give us good pilots to conduct us to the open seas; lift no false lights along the dangerous coasts, and if it shall please God to send us propitious winds, or fearful gales, we shall survive or perish as our energies or neglect shall determine. We ask no special favors, but we plead for justice. While we scorn unmanly dependence: in the name of God, the universal Father, we demand the right to live, and labor, and to enjoy the fruits of our toil. The good work which God has assigned for the ages to come, will be finished, when our national literature shall be so purified as to reflect a faithful and a just light upon the character and social habits of our race, and the brush, and pencil, and chisel, and Lyre of Art, shall refuse to lend their aid to scoff at the afflictions of the poor, or to caricature, or ridicule a long-suffering people. When caste and prejudice in Christian churches shall be utterly destroyed, and shall be regarded as totally unworthy of Christians, and at variance with the principles of the gospel. When the blessings of the Christian religion, and of sound, religious education, shall be freely offered to all, then, and not till then, shall the effectual labors of God's people and God's instruments cease.

If slavery has been destroyed merely from *necessity*, let every class be enfranchised at the dictation of *justice*. Then we shall have a Constitution that shall be reverenced by all: rulers who shall be honored, and revered, and a Union that shall be sincerely loved by a brave and patriotic people, and which can never be severed.

Great sacrifices have been made by the people; yet, greater still are demanded ere atonement can be made for our national sins. Eternal justice holds heavy mortgages against us, and will require the payment of the last farthing. We have involved ourselves in the sin of unrighteous gain, stimulated by luxury, and pride, and the love of power and oppression; and prosperity and peace can be purchased only by blood, and with tears of repentance. We have paid some of the fearful installments, but there are other heavy obligations to be met.

The great day of the nation's judgment has come, and who shall be able to stand? Even we, whose ancestors have suffered the afflictions which are inseparable from a condition of slavery, for the period of two centuries and a half, now pity our land and weep with those who weep.

Upon the total and complete destruction of this accursed sin depends the safety and perpetuity of our Republic and its excellent institutions.

Let slavery die. It has had a long and fair trial. God himself has pleaded against it. The enlightened nations of the earth have condemned it. Its death warrant is signed by God and man. Do not commute its sentence. Give it no respite, but let it be ignominiously executed.

Honorable Senators and Representatives! illustrious rulers of this great nation! I cannot refrain this day from invoking upon you, in God's name, the blessings of millions who were ready to perish, but to whom a new and better life has been opened by your humanity, justice, and patriotism. You have said, "Let the Constitution of the country be so amended that slavery and involuntary servitude shall no longer exist in the United States, except in punishment for crime." Surely, an act so sublime could not escape Divine notice: and doubtless the deed has been recorded in the archives of heaven. Volumes may be appropriated to your praise and renown in the history of the world. Genius and art may perpetuate the glorious act on canvass and in marble, but certain and more lasting monuments in commemoration of your decision are already erected in the hearts and memories of a grateful people.

The nation has begun its exodus from worse than Egyptian bondage; and I beseech you that you say to the people, "*that they go forward.*" With the assurance of God's favor in all things done in obedience to his righteous will, and guided by day and by night by the pillars of cloud and fire, let us not pause until we have reached the other and safe side of the stormy and crimson sea. Let freemen and patriots mete out complete and equal justice to all men, and thus prove to mankind the superiority of our Democratic, Republican Government.

Favored men, and honored of God as his instruments, speedily finish the work which he has given you to do. *Emancipate, Enfranchise, Educate, and give the blessings of the gospel to every American citizen.*

"Hear ye not how, from all high points of Time,—
From peak to peak adown the mighty chain
That links the ages—echoing sublime
A Voice Almighty—leaps one grand refrain.
12

Wakening the generations with a shout,
And trumpet-call of thunder—Come ye out!

"Out from old forms and dead idolatries;
From fading myths and superstitious dreams:
From Pharisaic rituals and lies,
And all the bondage of the life that seems!
Out—on the pilgrim path, of heroes trod,
Over earth's wastes, to reach forth after God!

"The Lord hath bowed his heaven, and come down!
Now, in this latter century of time,
Once more his tent is pitched on Sinai's crown!
Once more in clouds must Faith to meet him climb!
Once more his thunder crashes on our doubt
And fear and sin—'My people! come ye out!'

"From false ambitions and base luxuries;
From puny aims and indolent self-ends;
From cant of faith, and shams of liberties,
And mist of ill that Truth's pure day-beam bends:
Out, from all darkness of the Egypt-land,
Into my sun-blaze on the desert sand!

*    *    *    *    *    *

"Show us our Aaron, with his rod in flower!
Our Miriam, with her timbrel-soul in tune!
And call some Joshua, in the Spirit's power,
To poise our sun of strength at point of noon!
God of our fathers! over sand and sea,
Still keep our struggling footsteps close to thee!"*

Then before us a path of prosperity will open, and
upon us will descend the mercies and favors of God.
Then shall the people of other countries, who are
standing tip-toe on the shores of every ocean, earnestly looking to see the end of this amazing conflict,
behold a Republic that is sufficiently strong to out-

* Atlantic Monthly, 1862.

live the ruin and desolations of civil war, having the magnanimity to do justice to the poorest and weakest of her citizens. Thus shall we give to the world the form of a model Republic, founded on the principles of justice, and humanity, and Christianity, in which the burdens of war and the blessings of peace are equally borne and enjoyed by all.

THE END.

www.ingramcontent.com/pod-product-compliance
Lightning Source LLC
Chambersburg PA
CBHW021426090426
42742CB00009B/1274